Travellers' Greek

David Ellis is D and co-author o

Helen Rapi is cu

Dr John Baldwi University Colle

Other titles in the series

Travellers' Greek

D. L. Ellis, H. Rapi

Pronunciation Dr J. Baldwin

Pan Books London and Sydney

The publishers would like to thank the
National Tourist Organisation of Greece for their help
during the preparation of this book

First published 1981 by Pan Books Ltd,
Cavaye Place, London SW10 9PG
9 8
© D. L. Ellis and H. Rapi 1981
ISBN 0 330 26296 3
Printed and bound in Great Britain by
Hazell Watson & Viney Limited,
Member of the BPCC Group,
Aylesbury, Bucks

Contents

Using the phrase book

- This phrase book is designed to help you get by in Greece, to get what you want or need. It concentrates on the simplest but most effective way you can express these needs in an unfamiliar language.
- The CONTENTS on p. 5 gives you a good idea of which section to consult for the phrase you need.
- The INDEX on p. 155 gives more detailed information about where to look for your phrase.
- When you have found the right page you will be given:
  either – the exact phrase
  or   – help in making up a suitable sentence
  and   – help to get the pronunciation right
- The English sentences in **bold type** will be useful for you in a variety of different situations, so they are worth learning by heart. (See also DO IT YOURSELF, p. 142.)
- Wherever possible you will find help in understanding what Greek people are saying to *you*, in reply to your questions.
- If you want to practise the basic nuts and bolts of the language further, look at the DO IT YOURSELF section starting on p. 142.
- Note especially these three sections:
  Everyday expressions, p. 14
  Shop talk, p. 58
  Public notices, p. 119
  You are sure to want to refer to them most frequently.
- Once abroad, remember to make good use of the local tourist offices (see p. 27).

UK address:
The National Tourist Organization of Greece
195 Regent Street
London W1

A note on the pronunciation system and the Greek alphabet

It is usual in phrase books for there to be a pronunciation section, which tries to teach English-speaking tourists how to pronounce correctly the language of the country they are visiting. Such attempts are based on the argument that correct pronunciation is essential for comprehension. The system in this book, however, is founded on three quite different assumptions: Firstly, that it is not possible to describe in print the sounds of a foreign language in such a way that the English speaker with no phonetic training will produce them accurately, or even intelligibly; secondly, that perfect pronunciation is not essential for communication; and lastly, that the average visitor abroad is more interested in achieving successful communication than in learning how to pronounce new speech sounds. Observation and experience have shown these assumptions to be justified. The most important characteristic of the present system, therefore, is that it makes no attempt whatsoever to teach the sounds of the other language, but uses instead the nearest English sounds to them. The sentences transcribed for pronunciation are designed to be read as naturally as possible, as if they were ordinary English (of a generally south-eastern variety) and with no attempt to make the words sound 'foreign'. In this way you will still sound quite English but you will at the same time be understood. Practice always helps performance and it is a good idea to rehearse out loud any of the sentences you know you are going to need. When you come to the point of using them, say them with conviction.

In Greek it is important to stress or emphasize the syllables in *italics*, just as you would if we were to take as an English example: Little Jack Horner *sat* in the *corner*. Here we have ten syllables, but only four stresses. This is particularly important in Greek, as meaning can be dependent on stress and many words will be completely unintelligible to a Greek unless the stress is put in the correct place.

Of course you may enjoy trying to pronounce a foreign language as well as possible, and the present system is a good way to start. However, since it uses only the sounds of English, you will very soon need to depart from it as you begin to imitate the sounds you hear the native speaker produce and relate them to the spelling of the other language.

In the case of Greek there is a new alphabet to be learned which at first sight is likely to appear rather strange. However, if you are able to spend a little time studying it, you will find that it is in fact much simpler than our own alphabet! There are only twenty-four letters and the rules relating to their pronunciation are quite simple and regular. If you follow the guidelines below, you should be able to produce an intelligible rendering of any Greek word you see.

Printed	Handwritten	Name	Pronunciation
A α	*A a*	alfa	*a* as in f*a*ther, e.g. μαῦρος (m*a*vros) black
B β	*B b*	veeta	*v* as in *v*an, e.g. βαλίτσα (*v*aleetsa) suitcase
Γ γ	*Γ г*	gama	throaty *g; g* in *g*uild is quite acceptable, e.g. γάλα (*g*ala) milk. Before ε, η, ι, υ it becomes *y* e.g. γιά (*y*a) for
Δ δ	*Δ г*	delta	*th* as in *th*is and bro*th*er, e.g. δύο (*th*ee-o) two
E ε	*E ε*	epseelon	*e* as in g*e*t, e.g. ἐδῶ (eth*o*) here
Z ζ	*Z ʃ*	zeeta	*z* as in *z*oo, e.g. ζεστός (*z*estoss) hot
H η	*H η*	eeta	*ee* as in m*ee*t, e.g. ἠλεκτρικό (*ee*lektreeko) electricity supply
Θ θ	*Θ ϑ*	theeta	*th* as in *th*in, e.g. θέλω (*th*el-o) I want
I ι	*I ι*	eeota	*ee* as in m*ee*t, e.g. σπίτι (sp*ee*tee) house
K κ	*K к*	kapa	*k* as in *k*itten, e.g. καί (*k*eh) and
Λ λ	*Λ ʃ*	lambda	*l* as in *l*ive, e.g. λυπᾶμαι (*l*eepam-eh) I am sorry
M μ	*M μ*	mee	*m* as in *m*y, e.g. μέ (*m*eh) with
N ν	*N ν*	nee	*n* as in *n*ever, e.g. ναί (*n*eh) yes
Ξ ξ	*Ξ ξ*	ksee	*ks* as in tri*ck*s, e.g. ἔξι (e*ksee*) six
O o	*Ό o*	omeekron	*o* as in h*o*t, e.g. ὄνομα (*o*nomah) name

Printed	Handwritten	Name	Pronunciation
Π π	*Π ω*	pee	*p* as in *p*ie, e.g. πέντε (pendeh) five
Ρ ρ	*Ρ ρ*	ro	a semi-rolled *r* as in *r*ed, e.g. ρετσίνα (retseenah) resinated wine
Σ σ ς	*Σ σ*	seegma	*s* as in *s*end, e.g. στήθος (steethos) breast. Before β, γ, δ it becomes *z* but this is not very common. The form ς is used only at the end of a word
Τ τ	*Τ τ*	taf	*t* as in *t*op, e.g. Τρίτη (treetee) Tuesday
Υ υ	*Υ υ*	eepseelon	*ee* as in m*ee*t, e.g. μπύρα (beera) beer
Φ φ	*Φ φ*	fee	*f* as in *f*our, e.g. φιλμ (film) film
Χ χ	*Χ χ*	hee	*ch* as in lo*ch* or if you can't make this sound, a fairly forceful *h* as in *h*elp, e.g. χρόνος (hronoss) year
Ψ ψ	*Ψ ψ*	psee	*ps* as in to*ps*, e.g. ψάρι (psaree) fish
Ω ω	*Ω ω*	omega	*o* as in h*o*t, e.g. ὥρα (orah) hour, time

You have probably noticed that some of the letters are pronounced alike. They are Ηη Ιι Υυ pronounced *ee* as in m*ee*t, agr*ee* and Οο Ωω pronounced *o* as in h*o*t.

COMBINATIONS OF LETTERS

αι   *e* as in g*e*t, e.g. καί (k*e*h) and

αυ   *av* as in h*av*e, e.g. αὔριο (*av*reeo) tomorrow, but before
      voiceless consonants θ, κ, ξ, π, σ, τ, φ, χ, ψ pronounced *af*,
      e.g. αὐτό (*af*to) this

ει   *ee* as in m*ee*t, e.g. τρεῖς (tr*ee*ss) three

ευ   *ev* as in *ev*ent, e.g. Εὐρώπη (*ev*ropee) Europe, but before
      voiceless consonants θ, κ, ξ, π, σ, τ, φ, χ, ψ pronounced *ef*,
      e.g. εὐχαριστῶ (*ef*-har-eesto) thank you

οι   *ee* as in m*ee*t, e.g. κοινός (k*ee*noss) public

ου   *oo* as in f*oo*l, e.g. μπουκάλι (book*a*lee) bottle

γγ   *ng* as in a*ng*le, e.g. Ἀγγλία (a*ng*leea) England

γκ   *g* as in g*e*t, e.g. γκαρσόν (gars*o*n) waiter, but in the middle
      of a word *ng*, e.g. ἄγκυρα (a*ng*eera) anchor

γχ   *nh* as in e*nh*ance, e.g. μέ συγχωρεῖτε (meh see*nh*oreeteh)
      excuse me

μπ   *b* as in *b*ar, e.g. μπάρ (*b*ar) bar, but in the middle of a word
      sometimes *mb* as in λάμπα (la*mb*a) light bulb

ντ   *d* as in *d*ot, e.g. ντομάτα (*d*omata) tomato, but in the middle
      of a word *nd*, e.g. πέντε (pe*nd*eh) five

Note that the ' ', used where a word begins with a vowel have *no*
function in pronunciation and must therefore be ignored. The three
marks ` ´ ˜ all show one and the same thing, i.e. which syllable
carries stress; they have no other function.

καλή ἐπιτυχία!
kal*ee* epeeteeh*ee*a

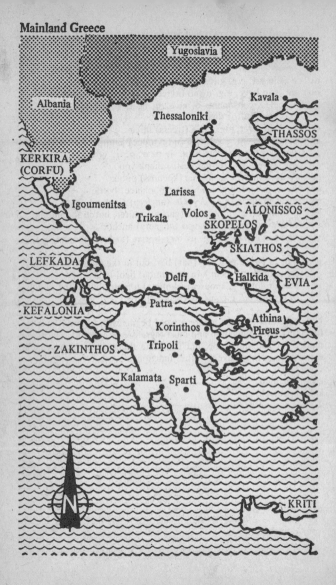

Mainland Greece

Mainland Greece and the islands

Bulgaria

Kavala

Alexandroupoli

THASSOS

ALONISSOS

SKOPELOS

LESVOS

Turkey

SKIATHOS

Halkida

EVIA

Athina
Pireus

SAMOS

MIKONOS

NAXOS

RODOS

KRITI

Iraklio

Everyday expressions

[See also 'Shop talk', p. 58]

Hello	Γειά σας
	yassas
Good morning ⎤	Καλημέρα
Good day ⎦	kal-eemehra
Good afternoon (after siesta) ⎤	Καλησπέρα
Good evening ⎦	kaleespera
Good night	Καληνύκτα
	kal-eeneekta
Goodbye	Γειά σας
	yassas
See you later	Θά σᾶς δῶ ἀργότερα
	tha sas tho argot-ehra
Yes	Ναί
	neh
Please	Παρακαλῶ
	parakalo
Yes, please	Ναί, παρακαλῶ
	neh, parakalo
Great!	ὡραῖα!
	oreh-a
Thank you	Εὐχαριστῶ
	ef-har-eesto
Thank you very much	Εὐχαριστῶ πάρα πολύ
	ef-har-eesto para pol-ee
That's right	Σωστό
	sosto
No	Ὄχι
	o-hee
No, thank you	Ὄχι, εὐχαριστῶ
	o-hee ef-har-eesto
I disagree	Διαφωνῶ
	thee-af-on-o
Excuse me ⎤	Συγγνώμη
Sorry ⎦	seeg-nom-ee
Don't mention it ⎤	Δέν πειράζει
That's OK ⎦	then peeraz-ee

That's good⎤ I like it ⎦	Αὐτό εἶναι καλό afto *ee*neh kal*o*
That's no good⎤ I don't like it ⎦	Δέν μ' ἀρέσει then mar-*es*-ee
I know	Ξέρω ksehr*o*
I don't know	Δέν ξέρω then ksehr*o*
It doesn't matter	Δέν πειράζει then peeraz-ee
Where's the toilet, please?	Ποῦ εἶναι ἡ τουαλέτα, παρακαλῶ; p*oo* een-eh ee too-al-*eh*-ta parakal*o*
How much is that? [*point*]	Πόσο κάνει ἐκεῖνο; p*o*sso kan-ee ekeen*o*
Is the service included?	Εἶναι μέ τό σερβίς; *ee*neh meh toh sehr-vee*ss*
Do you speak English?	Μιλᾶτε Ἀγγλικά; meelat-eh angleek*a*
I'm sorry . . .	Λυπᾶμαι ἀλλά . . . leepam-eh all*a* . . .
I don't speak Greek	δέν μιλῶ ἑλληνικά then meel*o* elleen-eek*a*
I only speak a little Greek	μιλῶ μόνο λίγα ἑλληνικά meel*o* mono leeg-a elleen-eek*a*
I don't understand	δέν καταλαβαίνω then kat-alav-en-o
Please can you . . .	Σᾶς παρακαλῶ, μπορεῖτε νά . . . sas parakal*o*, boreeteh na . . .
repeat that?	τό ἐπαναλάβετε αὐτό; toh ep-an-al*a*v-et-eh aft*o*
speak more slowly?	μιλᾶτε πιό ἀργά; meelat-eh pee-*o* arg*a*
write it down?	τό γράψετε; toh gr*a*pset-eh
What is this called in Greek? [*point*]	Πῶς τό λέτε στά Ἑλληνικά; p*o*ss toh let-eh sta elleen-eek*a*

Crossing the border

ESSENTIAL INFORMATION

- Don't waste time before you leave rehearsing what you're going to say to the border officials – the chances are that you won't have to say anything at all, especially if you travel by air.
- It's more useful to check that you have your documents handy for the journey: passport, tickets, money, travellers' cheques, insurance documents, driving licence and car registration documents.
- Look for these signs:
  ΤΕΛΩΝΕΙΟΝ (customs)
  ΣΥΝΟΡΑ (border)
  [For further signs and notices, see p. 119]
- You may be asked routine questions by the customs officials [see below]. If you have to give personal details see 'Meeting people', p. 18. The other important answer to know is 'Nothing': Τίποτα (teepota).

ROUTINE QUESTIONS

Passport?	Διαβατήριο; thee-av-ateerio
Insurance?	Ἀσφάλεια; as-fal-ya
Registration document? (logbook)	Ἄδεια κυκλοφορίας; athia keek-loforee-ass
Ticket, please	Τό εἰσιτήριο σας, παρακαλῶ toh eess-eeteerio sas parakalo
Have you anything to declare?	Ἔχετε νά δηλώσετε τίποτα; eh-het-eh na thee-loss-et-eh teepota
Where are you going?	Ποῦ πηγαίνετε; poo peeg-en-et-eh
How long are you staying?	Πόσο θά μείνετε; posso tha meenet-eh
Where have you come from?	Ἀπό ποῦ ἤρθατε; apo poo eerthat-eh

You may also have to fill in forms which ask for:

surname	επώνυμο
first name	ὄνομα
date of birth	ἡμερομηνία γεννήσεως
address	διεύθυνση
nationality	ἐθνικότης
profession	ἐπάγγελμα
passport number	ἀριθμός διαβατηρίου
issued at	ἐκδοθέν εἰς
place of birth	τόπος γεννήσεως
signature	ὑπογραφή

Meeting people

[See also 'Everyday expressions', p. 14]

Breaking the ice

Hello	Γειά σας
	yassas
Good morning	Καλημέρα
	kal-eemehra
How are you?	Πῶς εἴστε;
	poss eess-teh
Pleased to meet you	Χαίρω πολύ
	hehr-o pol-ee
I am here . . .	Εἶμαι ἐδῶ . . .
	eemeh eth-o . . .
on holiday	γιά διακοπές
	ya thee-ak-opess
on business	γιά δουλειά
	ya thool-ya
Can I offer you . . .	Μπορῶ νά σᾶς προσφέρω . . .
	boro na sas pross-fehro . . .
a drink?	ἕνα ποτό;
	enna pot-o
a cigarette?	ἕνα τσιγάρο;
	enna tseegar-o
a cigar?	ἕνα ποῦρο;
	enna poo-ro
Are you staying long?	Θά μείνετε πολύ;
	tha meenet-eh pol-ee

Name

What's your name?	Πῶς λέγεσται;
	poss leg-es-teh
My name is . . .	Μέ λένε . . .
	meh len-eh . . .

Family

Are you married?	Εἶστε παντρεμένος/παντρεμένη;* *ees–*teh pandrem-*en*-oss/ pandrem-*en*-ee*
I am ...	Εἶμαι ... *ee*meh ...
married	παντρεμένος/παντρεμένη* pandrem-*en*-oss/pandrem-*en*-ee*
single	ἀνύπαντρος/ἀνύπαντρη* an-*ee*pandr-oss/an-*ee*pandr-ee*
This is ...	Ἀπό ἐδῶ ... apo eth-*o* ...
my wife	ἡ συζυγός μου ee seezeeg*oz*moo
my husband	ὁ συζυγός μου o seezeeg*oz*moo
my son	ὁ γυιός μου o y*oz*moo
my daughter	ἡ κόρη μου ee k*o*reemoo
my (boy)friend	ὁ φίλος μου o f*ee*loz*moo
my (male) colleague	ὁ συνάδελφος μου o seen-*a*thelf-*oz*moo
my (female) colleague	ἡ συνάδελφος μου ee seen-*a*thelf-*oz*moo
Do you have any children?	Ἔχετε παιδιά; *eh*-het-eh peth-y*a*
I have ...	Ἔχω ... *eh*-ho ...
one daughter	μία κόρη *mee*-a k*o*ree
one son	ἔνα γυιό *en*na yo
two daughters	δύο κόρες *thee*-o k*o*ress
three sons	τρεῖς γυιούς tr*ee*ss y*oo*ss
No, I haven't any children	Ὄχι, δέν ἔχω παιδιά *o*-hee, then *eh*-ho peth-y*a*

*For men use the first alternative, for women the second.

Where you live

Are you Greek?	Εἴστε Ἕλληνας/Ἑλληνίδα;*
	ees-theh elleenas/elleen*ee*tha*
I am ...	Εἴμαι ...
	*ee*meh ...
American	Ἀμερικανός/Ἀμερικανίδα
	amerikan-*oss*/amerikan-*ee*tha*
English	Ἐγγλέζος/Ἐγγλέζα
	englez-oss/englez-a*

[For other nationalities, see p. 136]

Where are you from?

I am ...	Εἴμαι ...
	*ee*meh ...
from London	ἀπό τό Λονδῖνο
	apo toh lon-theeno
from England	ἀπό τήν Ἀγγλία
	apo teen anglee-a

[For other countries see p. 134]

from the north	ἀπό τό βορρᾶ
	apo toh vorra
from the south	ἀπό τό νότο
	apo toh not-o
from the east	ἀπό τήν ἀνατολή
	apo teen anatolee
from the west	ἀπό τή δύση
	apo tee theessee
from the centre	ἀπό τό κέντρο
	apo toh kendro

*For men use the first alternative, for women the second.

For the businessman and woman

I'm from . . . (firm's name)
Εἶμαι ἀπό . . .
eemeh ap*o* . . .

I have an appointment with . . .
Ἔχω ραντεβοῦ μέ . . .
eh-ho randev*oo* meh . . .

May I speak to . . .?
Μπορῶ νά μιλήσω στό . . .;
bor*o* na meel*ee*so sto . . .

This is my card
Ὁρίστε ἡ κάρτα μου
or*eest*-eh ee k*a*rta moo

I'm sorry I'm late
Μέ συγχωρεῖτε πού ἄργησα
meh seenhor-*eet*-eh poo arg-*ee*ssa

Can I fix another appointment?
Μπορῶ νά κλείσω ἄλλο ραντεβοῦ;
bor*o* na kl*ee*so *a*llo randev*oo*

I'm staying at the hotel (Delphi)
Μένω στό ξενοδοχεῖο (Δελφοί)
men-o sto ksen-otho-*hee*-o (Delph*i*)

I'm staying in (Stadium) Street
Μένω στήν ὁδό (Σταδίου)
men-o steen oth*o* (stath*ee*-oo)

Asking the way

ESSENTIAL INFORMATION

- Keep a look out for all these place names as you will find them on shops, maps and notices.

WHAT TO SAY

Excuse me, please

Μέ συγχωρεῖτε, παρακαλῶ
meh seenhor-*eet*-eh parakal*o*

How do I get ...

Πῶς μπορῶ νά πάω ...
p*o*ss bor*o* na p*a*-o ...

to Athens?

στήν Ἀθήνα;
steen ath*ee*na

to Ermou Street?

στήν ὁδό Ἑρμοῦ;
steen oth*o* ehrm*oo*

to the Hotel Caravel?

στό ξενοδοχεῖο Καραβέλ;
sto ksen-oth*o*-h*ee*-o karave*l*

to the airport?

στό ἀεροδρόμιο;
sto ehr-othr*o*m-yo

to the beach?

στή παραλία;
stee paral*ee*a

to the bus station?

στή στάση λεωφορείου;
stee st*a*ssee leh-ofor*ee*-oo

to the historic site?

στό ἱστορικό μνημεῖο;
sto eestoreek*o* mneem*ee*-o

to the market?

στήν ἀγορά;
.steen agor*a*

to the police station?

στήν ἀστυνομία;
steen asteen-om*ee*-a

to the port?

στό λιμάνι;
sto leeman-ee

to the post office?

στό ταχυδρομεῖο;
sto ta-hee-throm*ee*-o

to the railway station?

στό σιδηροδρομικό σταθμό;
sto see-theerothrom-eek*o* stathm*o*

to the sports stadium?

στό στάδιο;
sto stathio

to the tourist information office?	στό γραφείο πληροφοριῶν γιά τουρίστες; sto grafee-o pleerof-oree-on ya tooreest-ess
to the town centre?	στό κέντρο τῆς πόλης; sto kendro teess pol-eess
to the town hall?	στό δημαρχείο; sto theem-ar-hee-o
Excuse me, please	Μέ συγχωρείτε, παρακαλῶ meh seenhor-eet-eh parakalo
Is there . . . near by?	Ὑπάρχει ἐδῶ κοντά . . . eepar-hee eth-o konda . . .
an art gallery	πινακοθήκη; peen-akoth-eekee
a baker's	ἀρτοποιείο; artop-ee-ee-o
a bank	τράπεζα; trap-ez-a
a bar	μπάρ; bar
a botanical garden	βοτανικός κῆπος; vot-an-eekoss keeposs
a bus stop	στάση λεωφορείου; stassee leh-oforee-oo
a butcher's	κρεοπωλείο; kreh-opolee-o
a café	καφενείο kafen-eeo
a cake and coffee shop	ζαχαροπλαστείο; za-har-oplastee-o
a campsite	κατασκήνωση; kata-skeenossee
a car park	πάρκιγκ; parking
a change bureau	γραφείο συναλλάγματος; grafee-o seenal-agmat-oss
a chemist's	φαρμακείο; farma-kee-o
a church	ἐκκλησία; ek-leessee-a
a cinema	σινεμά; seenema

Is there . . . near by?

Ὑπάρχει ἐδῶ κοντά . . .
eepar-hee eth-*o* kond*a* . . .

a concert hall

αἴθουσα συναυλιῶν;
*e*h-thoossa seen-avli-*o*n

a delicatessen

ἐδωδιμοπωλεῖο;
eth-oth-eemopol*ee*-o

a dentist's

ὀδοντιατρεῖο;
othondi-atr*ee*-o

a department store

μεγάλο ἐμπορικό κατάστημα;
meh-g*a*l-o emboreek*o* kat*a*steema

a disco

ντισκοτέκ;
discoteque

a doctor's surgery

ἰατρεῖο;
ee-atr*ee*-o

a dry-cleaner's

στεγνοκαθαριστήριο;
stegno-kathar-eest*ee*rio

a fishmonger's

ψαράδικο;
psar*a*th-eek*o*

a garage (for repairs)

συνεργεῖο;
seenehr-g*ee*o

a hairdresser's

κομμωτήριο;
kommot-*ee*rio

a greengrocer's

μανάβικο;
man*a*v-eeko

a grocer's

μπακάλικο;
bak*a*l-eeko

a hardware shop

μαγαζί μέ σιδηρικά;
magaz-*ee* meh s*ee*th-eeree-k*a*

a hospital

νοσοκομεῖο;
nosokom*ee*-o

a hotel

ξενοδοχεῖο;
ksen-otho-h*ee*-o

a laundry

καθαριστήριο;
kathar-eest*ee*rio

a museum

μουσεῖο;
moss*ee*-o

a newsagent's

περίπτερο;
peh-r*ee*ptero

a nightclub

νάϊτ κλάμπ;
night club

a petrol station

βενζινάδικο;
venzeen-*a*theeko

a postbox	γραμματοκιβώτιο;
	grammatok-eev*ot*-yo
a toilet	τουαλέτα;
	too-al-*eh*-ta
a restaurant	ἑστιατόριο;
	estee-atorio
a snack bar	σνάκ μπάρ;
	snack bar
a sports ground	γήπεδο;
	y*ee*-pehtho
a supermarket	σούπερ μαρκέτ;
	supermarket
a sweet shop (kiosk)	περίπτερο;
	peh-r*ee*ptero
a swimming pool	πισίνα;
	pee-s*ee*na
a taxi stand	πιάτσα γιά ταξί;
	pee-*a*tsa ya taks*ee*
a public telephone	τηλέφωνο;
	teelef-ono
a theatre	θέατρο;
	theh-atro
a tobacconist's kiosk	περίπτερο;
	peh-r*ee*ptero
a travel agent's	πρακτορείο ταξιδιῶν;
	praktor*ee*-o takseethee-*on*
a youth hostel	ξενών νεότητος;
	ksen-*on* neh-*ot*-eetoss
a zoo	ζωολογικός κῆπος;
	zo-olog-eek*oss* k*ee*poss

DIRECTIONS

- Asking where a place is, or if a place is near by, is one thing; making sense of the answer is another.
- Here are some of the most important directions and replies.

Left	᾽Αριστερά
	areesteh-r*a*
Right	Δεξιά
	theksy*a*
Straight on	῎Ισια
	*ee*sia

There	Ἐκεῖ
	ek-*ee*
First left/right	Ὁ πρῶτος δρόμος ἀριστερά/δεξιά
	o prot-oss throm-oss areesteh-ra/ theksya
Second left/right	Ὁ δεύτερος δρόμος ἀριστερά/δεξιά
	o thefteross throm-oss areesteh-ra/ theksya
At the crossroads	Στό σταυροδρόμι
	sto stavro-thromee
At the traffic lights	Στά φανάρια
	sta fanar-ee-a
At the roundabout	Στή πλατεῖα
	stee plat-*ee*a
At the level-crossing	Στή διασταύρωση
	stee thee-astavro-see
It's near/far	Εἶναι κοντά/μακριά
	*ee*neh konda/makree-*a*
One kilometre	Ἕνα χιλιόμετρο
	enna heelee-*o*metro
Two kilometres	Δύο χιλιόμετρα
	thee-o heelee-*o*metra
Five minutes . . .	Πέντε λεπτά . . .
	pendeh lept*a* . . .
on foot	μέ τά πόδια
	meh ta poth-ya
by car	μέ τό αὐτοκίνητο
	meh toh aftok-*ee*neeto
Take . . .	Πάρτε . . .
	parteh . . .
the bus	τό λεωφορεῖο
	toh leh-of-or*ee*-o
the ferry-boat	τό φέρυ μπώτ
	toh ferry-boat
the train	τό τραῖνο
	toh tren-o
the trolley-bus	τό τρόλλεϋ
	toh troll-ee
the underground	τόν ἠλεκτρικό
	ton eelektreek-*o*

[*For public transport, see p. 110*]

The tourist information office

ESSENTIAL INFORMATION

- Almost all towns in Greece have a tourist information office. Most towns have a Tourist Police, who control prices, inspect facilities and assist tourists generally. All road border control posts have an information desk.
- Look out for these words:
  ΓΡΑΦΕΙΟ ΕΛΛΗΝΙΚΟΥ ΟΡΓΑΝΙΣΜΟΥ ΤΟΥΡΙΣΜΟΥ (Greek Tourist Organization – ΕΟΤ)
  ΤΟΥΡΙΣΤΙΚΗ ΑΣΤΥΝΟΜΙΑ (Tourist Police)
- These offices give you free information in the form of printed leaflets, foldouts, brochures, lists and plans.
- You may have to pay for some types of document.
- For finding a tourist office, see p. 22

WHAT TO SAY

Please have you got . . .	Παρακαλῶ, ἔχετε . . . parakalo eh-het-eh . . .
a plan of the town?	ἕνα χάρτη τῆς πόλης; enna hartee teess pol-eess
a list of hotels?	μία λίστα μέ ξενοδοχεῖα; mee-a leesta meh ksen-otho-hee-a
a list of campsites?	μία λίστα μέ κατασκηνώσεις; mee-a leesta meh kataskeen-osseess
a list of restaurants?	μία λίστα μέ ἑστιατόρια; mee-a leesta meh estee-atoria
a list of coach excursions?	μία λίστα μέ ἐκδρομές μέ πούλμαν; mee-a leesta meh ek-throm-ess meh poolman
a list of events?	μία λίστα μέ ἐκδηλώσεις; mee-a leesta meh ek-thee-losseess
a leaflet on the town?	ἕνα φυλλάδιο γιά τήν πόλη; enna feellath-yo ya teen pol-ee
a leaflet on the region?	ἕνα φυλλάδιο γιά τήν περιοχή; enna feelath-yo ya teen peri-ohee

Please have you got . . .	Παρακαλῶ, ἔχετε . . .
	parakalo eh-het-eh . . .
a railway timetable?	τά δρομολόγια γιά τά τραῖνα;
	ta thromolo-ya ya ta tren-a
a bus timetable?	τά δρομολόγια γιά τά λεωφορεῖα;
	ta thromolo-ya ya ta leh-of-oree-a
In English, please	Στ' Ἀγγλικά, σᾶς παρακαλῶ
	stangleeka sas parakalo
How much do I owe you?	Πόσο σᾶς ὀφείλω;
	posso sas ofeelo
Can you recommend . . .	Μπορεῖτε νά μοῦ προτείνετε . . .
	boreeteh na moo proteenet-eh . . .
a cheap hotel?	ἕνα φθηνό ξενοδοχεῖο;
	enna ftheeno ksen-otho-hee-o
a cheap restaurant?	ἕνα φθηνό ἑστιατόριο;
	enna ftheeno es-tee-atorio
Can you book a room/a table for me?	Μπορεῖτε νά μοῦ κλείσετε ἕνα δωμάτιο/ἕνα τραπέζι;
	boreeteh na moo kleesset-eh enna thomat-yo/enna trap-ez-ee

LIKELY ANSWERS

You need to understand when the answer is 'No'. You may not be able to tell by the assistant's facial expression, tone of voice and gesture as these are quite different from those you will be used to; but there are some language clues, such as:

No	Ὄχι
	o-hee
I'm sorry	Λυπᾶμαι
	leepam-eh
I don't have a list of campsites	Δέν ἔχω λίστα μέ κατασκηνώσεις
	then eh-ho leesta meh kataskeen-osseess
I haven't got any left	Δέν ἔχω ἄλλες
	then eh-ho alless
It's free	Εἶναι τσάμπα
	eeneh tsa-ba

Accommodation

Hotel

ESSENTIAL INFORMATION

- If you want hotel-type accommodation, all the following words in capital letters are worth looking for on name boards:
  ΞΕΝΟΔΟΧΕΙΟ (hotel)
  ΜΟΤΕΛ (motel)
  ΕΝΟΙΚΙΑΖΟΝΤΑΙ ΔΩΜΑΤΙΑ (rooms to let)
  ΞΕΝΙΑ (luxurious hotels and usually more expensive than ordinary hotels)
- A list of hotels in the town or district can usually be obtained at the local tourist office or at the local Tourist Police or police station. These lists are also available from the National Tourist Organization of Greece in London [see p. 7].
- Recommended hotels are classified into six categories: De luxe or AA and 1st to 5th class or A to E.
- The cost is displayed in the room itself; so you can check it when having a look around before agreeing to stay.
- The displayed cost is for the room itself, per night and not per person. Breakfast is extra and therefore optional.
- In small hotels and village rooms breakfast is paid for separately, if available.
- A Greek breakfast will usually consist of a cup of coffee or tea with bread, butter and jam or honey.
- A service charge of 15% is usually included in the bill but tipping is optional.
- Your passport is requested when registering at a hotel and will normally be kept overnight.
- Finding a hotel, see. p. 22.

WHAT TO SAY

I have a booking	Ἔχω κλείσει ἕνα δωμάτιο
	eh-ho kleessee enna thomat-yo
Have you any vacancies, please?	Ἔχετε δωμάτια, παρακαλῶ;
	eh-het-eh thomat-ya parakalo
Can I book a room?	Μπορῶ νά κλείσω ἕνα δωμάτιο;
	boro na kleeso enna thomat-yo

It's for . . .

Εἶναι γιά . . .
eeneh ya . . .

one person
ἕνα ἄτομο
enna atomo

two people
δύο ἄτομα
thee-o atoma

[*For numbers, see p. 125*]

It's for . . .

Εἶναι γιά . . .
eeneh ya . . .

one night
μία βραδιά
mee-a vrath-ya

two nights
δύο βραδιές
thee-o vrath-yes

one week
μία βδομάδα
mee-a vthoma-tha

two weeks
δύο βδομάδες
thee-o vthomath-ess

I would like . . .
Θά ἤθελα . . .
tha eethella . . .

a (quiet) room
ἕνα (ἥσυχο) δωμάτιο
enna (eessee-ho) thomat-yo

two rooms
δύο δωμάτια
thee-o thomat-ya

with a single bed
μέ ἕνα μονό κρεββάτι
meh enna mono krevvat-ee

with two single beds
μέ δύο μονά κρεββάτια
meh thee-o mona krevvat-ya

with a double bed
μέ ἕνα διπλό κρεββάτι
meh enna theeplo krevvat-ee

with a toilet
μέ τουαλέτα
meh too-al-eh-ta

with a bathroom
μέ μπάνιο
meh ban-yo

with a shower
μέ ντούς
meh dooss

with a cot
μέ παιδικό κρεββάτι
meh peh-theeko krevvat-ee

with a balcony
μέ μπαλκόνι
meh balkon-ee

Do you serve meals?
Σερβίρετε γεύματα;
sehrveer-et-eh gevmata

At what time is ...	Τί ὥρα σερβίρετε ... tee ora serv-*eer*-et-eh ...
breakfast?	τό πρωινό; toh pro-*ee*no
lunch?	τό γεύμα; toh gevma
dinner?	τό δεῖπνο; toh th*ee*pno
How much is it?	Πόσο κάνει; posso kanee
Can I look at the room?	Μπορῶ νά δῶ τό δωμάτιο; boro na tho toh thom*a*t-yo
I'd prefer a room ...	Θά προτιμοῦσα ἕνα δωμάτιο ... tha proteem-*oo*ssa enna thom*a*t-yo ...
at the front/at the back	μπροστά/πίσω brosta/p*ee*sso
OK, I'll take it	Ἐντάξει, θά τό πάρω end*a*ksee tha toh par-o
No thanks, I won't take it	Ὄχι εὐχαριστῶ, δέν θά τό πάρω o-hee ef-har-ee*sto* then tha toh par-o.
The key to number (10), please	Τό κλειδί γιά τό νούμερο (δέκα), παρακαλῶ toh kleeth*ee* ya toh n*oo*mero (th*ek*-a) parakalo
Please, may I have ...	Νά μοῦ δώσετε ... na moo thoh-set-eh ...
a coat hanger?	μία κρεμάστρα; mee-a kreh-mastra
a towel?	μία πετσέτα; mee-a petset-a
a glass?	ἕνα ποτήρι; enna pot-*ee*ree
some soap?	ἕνα σαπούνι; enna sap*oo*nee
an ashtray?	ἕνα τασάκι; enna tasahkee
another pillow?	ἄλλο ἕνα μαξιλάρι; allo enna maks-eelaree
another blanket?	ἄλλη μία κουβέρτα; allee mee-a koo-vehr-ta

Come in!	Περᾶστε! peh-rasteh
One moment, please!	Ἕνα λεπτό, σᾶς παρακαλῶ! enna lepto sas parakalo
Please can you . . .	Μπορεῖτε παρακαλῶ νά . . . boreeteh parakalo na . . .
do this laundry/dry cleaning?	πλύνετε αὐτό στό πλυντήριο/ στεγνοκαθαριστήριο; pleenet-eh afto sto pleendeerio/ stegno-kathar-eesteerio
call me at . . .?	μέ τηλεφωνήσετε στίς . . .; meh teelef-on-eesset-eh steess . . .
help me with my luggage?	μέ βοηθήσετε μέ τά πράγματα; meh vo-eeth-eesset-eh meh ta pragmatah
call me a taxi for . . .?	καλέσετε ἕνα ταξί γιά . . .; kal-esset-eh enna taksee ya . . .

[For times, see p. 127]

The bill, please	Τό λογαριασμό, παρακαλῶ toh logaree-azmo parakalo
Is service included?	Εἶναι μέ τό σερβίς; eeneh meh toh serveess
I think this is wrong	Νομίζω πώς αὐτό εἶναι λάθος nom-eezo poss afto eeneh lath-oss
May I have a receipt?	Μπορῶ νά ἔχω μία ἀπόδειξη; boro na ehho mee-a apoth-eeksee

At breakfast

Some more . . . please	Καί ἄλλο . . . παρακαλῶ keh allo . . . parakalo
coffee	καφέ kaf-eh
tea	τσάϊ tsa-ee
bread	ψωμί psom-ee
butter	βούτυρο vooteero
honey	μέλι mel-ee

Some more jam	Καί ἄλλη μαρμελάδα
	keh allee marmelatha
May I have a boiled egg?	Νά πάρω ἕνα βραστό αὐγό;
	nah paro enna vrasto avgo

LIKELY REACTIONS

Have you an identity document, please?	Ἔχετε ταυτότητα, παρακαλῶ;
	eh-het-eh taftot-eeta parakalo
What's your name?	Πῶς λέγεσται;
	poss legesteh
Sorry, we're full	Λυπᾶμαι, δέν ἔχουμε δωμάτιο
	leepam-eh then eh-hoomeh thomat-yo
I haven't any rooms left	Δέν ἔχουμε δωμάτια
	then eh-hoomeh thomat-ya
Do you want to have a look?	Θέλετε νά ρίξετε μία ματιά;
	thel-et-eh na reekset-eh mee-a mat-ya
How many people is it for?	Γιά πόσα ἄτομα εἶναι;
	ya possa atoma een-eh
We only serve breakfast	Σερβίρουμε πρωινό μόνο
	serv-eer-oom-eh pro-een-o mon-o
From (seven o'clock) onwards	Μετά τίς (ἑπτά)
	met-a teess (epta)
From (midday) onwards	Μετά τίς (δώδεκα)
	met-a teess (thoth-eka)

[For times, see p. 127]

It's (200) drachmas	(διακόσες) δραχμές
	(thee-akoss-ess) thra-hmess

[For numbers, see p. 125]

Camping and youth hostelling

ESSENTIAL INFORMATION

Camping

- Look for the word: ΚΑΜΠΙΝΓΚ (camping) or this sign.
  Note μ = metres.

- Be prepared for the following charges:
  per person
  for the car (if applicable)
  for the tent or caravan plot
  for electricity
  for hot showers
- A reduction of 10% is made to the holders of AIT or FIA membership cards.
- You must provide proof of identity, such as your passport.
- Passports or identity cards can be returned to their holders only on settlement of the account.
- For the NTOG camping sites, which are better organized, advanced booking is strongly recommended.
- Camping is tolerated almost anywhere outside built-up areas but it is always best to get the landowner's permission beforehand. The police have the right to forbid you camping off-site in case of overcrowding, poor hygiene etc.

Youth hostels

- Look for the word: ΞΕΝΩΝ ΝΕΟΤΗΤΟΣ (youth hostel) or the sign shown on the next page.

- The charge per night is the same everywhere.
- You must have a YHA card.
- Accommodation is in dormitories.
- In most youth hostels there are cafeterias where light meals and drinks can be bought at reasonable prices.
- For finding a campsite and youth hostel, see p. 22.
- For buying or replacing camping equipment, see p. 56.

WHAT TO SAY

I have a booking	Ἔχω κρατήσει θέση
	eh-ho krateé-see thessee
Have you any vacancies?	Ἔχετε θέσεις;
	eh-het-eh thesseess
It's for . . .	Εἶναι γιά . . .
	eeneh ya . . .
one adult/one person	ἔναν ἐνήλικο/ἔνα ἄτομο
	ennan en-eeleeko/enna atomo
two adults/two people	δύο ἐνήλικες/δύο ἄτομα
	thee-o en-eeleekess/thee-o atoma
and one child	καί ἔνα παιδί
	keh enna peth-ee
and two children	καί δύο παιδιά
	keh theeo peth-ya
It's for . . .	Εἶναι γιὰ . . .
	eeneh ya . . .
one night	μία βραδιά
	mee-a vrath-ya
two nights	δύο βραδιές
	thee-o vrath-yes
one week	μία βδομάδα
	mee-a vthoma-tha
two weeks	δύο βδομάδες
	thee-o vthomath-ess

How much is it . . . | Πόσο κάνει . . .
posso kan-ee . . .

    for the tent? | ἡ σκηνή;
ee skee*nee*

    for the caravan? | τό κάραβαν;
toh karavan

    for the car? | τό αὐτοκίνητο;
toh aftokeen-ee*to*

    for the electricity? | τό ἠλεκτρικό;
toh eelek-tree*ko*

    per person? | τό ἄτομο;
toh *a*tomo

    per day/night? | τή μέρα/βραδιά;
tee meh-ra/vrath-y*a*

May I look round? | Μπορῶ νά ρίξω μιά ματιά;
boro na reekso mee-a mat-y*a*

Do you close the gate at night? | Κλειδώνετε τήν πόρτα τή νύκτα;
kleethon-et-eh teen porta tee neehta

Do you provide anything . . . | Σερβίρετε . . .
sehr-veer-et-eh . . .

    to eat? | φαγητό;
fag-eet*o*

. to drink? | ποτά;
pot*a*

Is there/are there . . . | Ἔχετε . . .
eh-het-eh . . .

    a bar | μπάρ;
bar

    hot showers? | ζεστά ντούς;
zesta doo*ss*

    a kitchen? | κουζίνα;
koozeena

    a laundry? | πλυντήριο;
pleendeerio

    a restaurant? | ἐστιατόριο;
estee-ator*io*

    a shop? | μαγαζί;
magaz-*ee*

    a swimming pool? | πισίνα;
peeseena

[*For food shopping, see p. 63, and for eating and drinking out, see p. 79*]

Where are . . .	Πού εἶναι . . .
	poo eeneh . . .
the dustbins?	οἱ σκουπιδοτενεκέδες;
	ee skoo-peethoten-ek-eth-ess
the showers?	τά ντούς;
	ta dooss
the toilets?	οἱ τουαλέτες;
	ee too-al-et-ess
At what time must one . . .	Τί ὥρα πρέπει . . .
	tee ora prehpee . . .
go to bed?	νά κοιμηθοῦμε;
	na keemeethoom-eh
get up?	νά ξυπνήσουμε;
	na kseep-neessoom-eh
Please have you got . . .	Ἔχετε . . . παρακαλῶ
	eh-het-eh . . . *parakalo*
a broom?	μία σκούπα;
	mee-a skoopa
a corkscrew?	ἕνα ἀνοικτήρι;
	enna an-eekteeree
a drying-up cloth?	μία πετσέτα γιά τά πιάτα;
	mee-a petset-a ya ta pee-at-a
a fork?	ἕνα πηρούνι;
	enna pee-roonee
a fridge?	ψυγεῖο;
	pseeg-ee-o
a frying pan?	ἕνα τηγάνι;
	enna teegan-ee
an iron?	ἕνα σίδερο;
	enna seethero
a knife?	ἕνα μαχαίρι;
	enna ma-he-ree
a plate?	ἕνα πιάτο;
	enna pee-at-o
a saucepan?	μία κατσαρόλα;
	mee-a katsarol-a
a teaspoon?	ἕνα κουταλάκι;
	enna koot-alak-ee
a tin opener?	ἕνα ἀνοικτήρι γιά κονσέρβες;
	enna aneek-teeree ya kon-sehr-vess
any washing powder?	σκόνη πλυσίματος;
	skon-ee pleess-eemat-oss
any washing-up liquid?	ὑγρό γιά τά πιάτα;
	eegro ya ta pee-at-a

The bill, please	Τό λογαριασμό, παρακαλῶ
	toh logaree-azmo parakalo

Problems

The toilet	Ἡ τουαλέτα
	ee too-al-*et*-a
The shower	Τό ντούς
	toh d*ooss*
The tap	Ἡ βρύση
	ee vr*ee*ssee
The razor point	Ἡ πρίζα γιά τή ξυριστική μηχανή
	ee pr*ee*za ya tee kseer-eesteek-*ee* mee-han-*ee*
The light	Τό φῶς
	toh f*oss*
. . . is not working	. . . χάλασε
	. . . h*al*-ass-eh
My camping gas has run out	Ἡ φιάλη ὑγραερίου τελείωσε
	ee fee-*al*-ee eegra-ehr-*ee*-oo tel*ee*-osseh
The bill, please	Τό λογαριασμό, παρακαλῶ
	toh logaree-azmo parakalo

LIKELY REACTIONS

Have you an identity document?	Ἔχετε ταυτότητα; eh-het-eh taftot-eeta
Your membership card, please	Τήν κάρτα σας, παρακαλῶ teen karta sas parakalo
What's your name?	Πῶς ὀνομάζεστε; poss on-omaz-es-teh
Sorry, we're full	Λυπᾶμαι, ἀλλά δέν ἔχουμε θέση leepam-eh alla then ehoomeh thessee
How many people is it for?	Γιά πόσα ἄτομα εἶναι; ya possa atoma eeneh
How many nights is it for?	Γιά πόσες βραδιές εἶναι; ya possess vrath-yes eeneh
It's (80) drachmas ...	(Ὀγδόντα) δραχμές ... (ogthonda) thra-hmess ...
per day/per night	τή μέρα/τή βραδιά tee meh-ra/tee vrath-ya

Rented accommodation: problem solving

ESSENTIAL INFORMATION

- If you're looking for accommodation to rent, look out for:
  ΕΝΟΙΚΙΑΖΕΤΑΙ (to let)
  ΔΙΑΜΕΡΙΣΜΑΤΑ (flats)
  ΔΩΜΑΤΙΑ (rooms)
  ΜΠΑΓΚΑΛΟΟΥΣ (bungalows)
- For arranging details of your let, see 'Hotel', p. 29.
- Key words you will meet if renting on the spot:
  μία προκαταβολή   deposit
  mee-a pro-katavol-ee
  τό κλειδί   key
  toh kleethee
- Having arranged your own accommodation and arrived with the key, check the obvious basics that you take for granted at home.
  Electricity: Voltage? Razors and small appliances brought from home may need adjusting. You may need an adaptor.
  Gas: Outside Athens, there is only bottled gas, and this is always butane gas.
  Cooker: Don't be surprised to find:
    – the grill inside the oven, or no grill at all
    – a lid covering the rings which lifts up to form a 'splashback'
  Toilet: Don't flush disposable nappies or anything else down the toilet, since the pipes are narrow and block easily. A bin is always provided.
  Water: Find the stopcock. Check taps and plugs – they may not operate in the way you are used to. Check how to turn on (or light) the hot water.
  Windows: Check the method of opening and closing windows and shutters.
  Insects: Is an insecticide spray provided? If not, get one locally.
  Equipment: See p. 56 for buying or replacing equipment.
- You will probably have an official agent, but be clear in your own mind who to contact in an emergency, even if it is only a neighbour in the first place.

WHAT TO SAY

My name is . . .	Ὀνομάζομαι . . . on-om*az*-om-eh . . .
I'm staying at . . .	Μένω στό . . . men-o sto . . .
They've cut off . . .	Ἔκοψαν . . . ek-opsan . . .
the electricity	τό ἠλεκτρικό toh eelek-treek*o*
the gas	τό γκάζι toh *g*azee
the water	τό νερό toh neh-r*o*
Is there . . . in the area?	Ὑπάρχει . . . στή περιοχή eepar-hee . . . stee peri-oh*ee*
an electrician	ἠλεκτρολόγος; eelektro-l*o*g-oss
a plumber	ὑδραυλικός; eethrav-leek*o*ss
Where is . . .	Ποῦ εἶναι . . . poo *ee*neh . . .
the fuse box?	ἡ ἀσφάλεια; ee asf*a*l-ya
the stopcock?	ὁ διακόπτης τοῦ νεροῦ; o thee-ak-*o*pteess too nehr-*oo*
the water heater?	τό θερμοσίφωνο; toh thermoss-*ee*fon-o
Is there central heating?	Ὑπάρχει καλοριφέρ; eepar-hee kaloreef*e*r
The cooker	Ἡ κουζίνα ee kooz*ee*na
The hair dryer	Τό σεσουάρ toh seh-soo-*ar*
The heating	Ἡ θέρμανση ee thehr-man-see
The immersion heater	Τό θερμοσίφωνο toh thermo-s*ee*fon-o
The iron	Τό σίδερο toh s*ee*thero
The refrigerator	Τό ψυγεῖο toh pseeg-*ee*-o

The telephone	Τό τηλέφωνο
	Toh teelef-on-o
The toilet	Ἡ τουαλέτα
	ee too-al-et-a
The washing machine	Τό πλυντήριο
	toh pleendeerio
. . . is not working	. . . χάλασε
	. . . hal-ass-eh
Where can I get . . .	Ποῦ μπορῶ νά βρῶ . . .
	poo boro na vro . . .
an adaptor for this?	ἕνα μετασχηματιστή γιά αὐτό;
	enna met-ass-hee-mat-ees-tee ya afto
a bottle of gas?	μία φιάλη γκάζι;
	mee-a fee-al-ee gazee
a fuse?	μία ἀσφάλεια;
	mee-a asfalya
an insecticide spray?	ἕνα ἐντομοκτόνο;
	enna endomokton-o
a light bulb	μία λάμπα;
	mee-a lamba
The drain	Ἡ ἀποχέτευση
	ee apo-het-ef-see
The sink	Ὁ νεροχύτης
	o nehro-heeteess
The toilet	Ἡ τουαλέτα
	ee too-al-et-a
. . . is blocked	. . . βούλωσε
	. . . vooloss-eh
The gas is leaking	Ὑπάρχει διαρροή γκάζι
	eepar-hee thee-arro-ee gazee
Can you mend it straightaway?	Μπορεῖτε νά τό ἐπισκευάσετε ἀμέσως;
	boreeteh na toh ep-eeskev-asset-eh a-mes-oss
When can you mend it?	Πότε θά τό ἐπισκευάσετε;
	pot-eh tha toh ep-eeskev-asset-eh
How much do I owe you?	Πόσο σᾶς ὀφείλω;
	posso sas ofeelo
When is the rubbish collected?	Πότε περνάει ὁ σκουπιδιάρης;
	pot-eh pehr-na-ee o skoopeeth-yar-eess

LIKELY REACTIONS

What's your name?	Πῶς λέγεσται; poss legesteh
What's your address?	Ποία εἶναι ἡ διεύθυνση σας; pee-a eeneh ee thee-ef-theen-see sas
There's a shop . . .	Ὑπάρχει μαγαζί . . . eeparhee magaz-ee . . .
in town	στήν πόλη steen pol-ee
in the village	στό χωριό sto horee-o
I can't come . . .	Δέν μπορῶ νά ἔρθω . . . then boro na ehr-tho . . .
today	σήμερα seemera
this week	αὐτή τή βδομάδα aftee tee vthoma-tha
until Monday	πρίν τή Δευτέρα preen tee thef-tehra
I can come . . .	Μπορῶ νά ἔρθω . . . boro na ehr-tho . . .
on Tuesday	τή Τρίτη tee treetee
when you want	ὅποτε θέλετε op-ot-eh thel-et-eh
Every day	Κάθε μέρα kath-eh mehra
Every other day	Μέρα παρά μέρα mehra para mehra
On (Wednesdays)	Κάθε (Τετάρτη) kath-eh (tet-artee)

[*For days of the week, see p. 129*]

General shopping

The chemist's

ESSENTIAL INFORMATION

- Look for the word ΦΑΡΜΑΚΕΙΟΝ (chemist's) or this sign.
- Medicines (drugs) are only available at a chemist's. Some non-drugs can be bought at a supermarket or department store, of course.
- Try the chemist before going to a doctor: they are usually qualified to treat minor injuries.
- Chemists take it in turns to stay open all night and on Sundays. A chemist's will display an illuminated list of all-night chemists (ΔΙΑΝΥΚΤΕΡΕΥΟΝΤΑ ΦΑΡΜΑΚΕΙΑ).
- Normal opening times are: 8.00 a.m. to 1.00 p.m. and 5.30 p.m. to 8.30 p.m. but you can check with the local tourist office.
- If you don't have insurance, you can be offered free medical service in certain state hospitals provided you can prove that you are uninsured and unable through personal financial means to cover the expenses of the medical treatment. However, this service is *extremely* limited and it is very unwise not to be properly insured.
- Some toiletries can also be bought at a ΚΑΤΑΣΤΗΜΑ ΚΑΛΛΥΝΤΙΚΩΝ (perfumery)
- Finding a chemist, see p. 22

WHAT TO SAY

I'd like ...	Θά ἤθελα ... tha eethella ...
some Alka Seltzer	αλκασέλτζερ alka seltzer
some antiseptic	ἕνα ἀντισηπτικό enna antee-seepteeko
some aspirin	ἕνα κουτί ἀσπιρίνες enna kootee aspeer-eeness
some bandage	ἕνα ἐπίδεσμο enna ep-eethezmo
some cotton wool	ἕνα βαμβάκι enna vamvak-ee
some eye drops	σταγόνες γιά τά μάτια stagon-ess ya ta mat-ya
some foot powder	ποῦδρα γιά τά πόδια poothra ya ta poth-ya
some gauze dressing	μερικές γάζες mehr-eekess gaz-ess
some inhalant	κάτι γιά εἰσπνοές kat-ee ya eess-pno-ess
some insect repellent	ἕνα ἐντομοκτόνο enna endomokton-o
some lip salve	μία ἀλοιφή γιά τά χείλη mee-a al-eefee ya ta heelee
some nose drops	σταγόνες γιά τή μύτη stagon-ess ya tee meetee
some sticking plaster	ἕνα λευκοπλάστη enna lefkoplastee
some throat pastilles	παστίλλιες γιά τό λαιμό pasteel-ee-ess ya toh lem-o
some Vaseline	μία βαζελίνη mee-a vaz-el-eenee
I'd like something for ...	Θά ἤθελα κάτι γιά ... tha eethella kat-ee ya ...
bites	τσίμπημα tseem-beema
burns	ἔγκαυμα engavma
chilblains	χιονίστρες hee-on-eestress

I'd like something for . . . Θά ἤθελα κάτι γιά . . .
tha eethella kat-ee ya . . .

a cold ἕνα κρύωμα
enna kreeoma

constipation δυσκοιλιότητα
theeskeelee-ot-eeta

a cough τόν βῆχα
ton vee-ha

diarrhoea διάρροια
thee-arria

earache πόνο στό αὐτί
pon-o sto aftee

flu γρίππη
greepee

scalds κάψιμο
kapseemo

sore gums σπυράκια
speerak-ya

sprains στραμπούλημα
stram-booleegma

stings κεντρίσματα
ken-dreezmata

sunburn ἔγκαυμα ἡλίου
engavma eelee-oo

sea/travel sickness ναυτία
naftee-a

I need . . . Χρειάζομαι . . .
hreeazomeh . . .

some baby food βρεφική τροφή
vrefeekee trof-ee

some contraceptives προφυλακτικά
prof-eelak-teeka

some deodorant ἕνα ἀποσμητικό
enna ap-ozmee-teeko

some disposable nappies πάνες μίας χρήσεως
pan-ess mee-ass hreess-eh-oss

some handcream μία κρέμα γιά τά χέρια
mee-a krem-a ya ta hehria

some lipstick ἕνα κραγιόν
enna kra-yon

some make-up remover	βαμβάκι γιά τόν καθαρισμό τοῦ προσώπου vamvak-ee ya ton kathar-eezmo too prossop-oo
some paper tissues	χαρτομάνδηλα hart-oman-theela
some razor blades	ξυραφάκια kseer-afak-ya
some safety pins	παραμάνες paraman-ess
some sanitary towels	σερβιέτες ὑγείας sehr-vee-et-ess eeg-ee-ass
some shaving cream	μία ξυριστική κρέμα mee-a kseer-eesteek-ee krem-a
some soap	ἕνα σαποῦνι enna sap-oonee
some suntan lotion/oil	μία ἀντιηλιακή κρέμα/λάδι mee-a antee-eelee-ak-ee krem-a/lathee
some talcum powder	ἕνα τάλκ enna talc
some Tampax	ἕνα ταμπάξ enna tampax
some toilet paper	ἕνα χαρτί ὑγείας enna hartee ee-yee-ass
some toothpaste	μία ὀδοντόκρεμα mee-a othond-okrem-a

[For other essential expressions, see 'Shop talk', p. 58]

Holiday items

ESSENTIAL INFORMATION

- Places to shop at and signs to look for:
  ΒΙΒΛΙΟΠΩΛΕΙΟ (bookshop)
  ΧΑΡΤΟΠΩΛΕΙΟ (stationery)
  ΦΩΤΟΓΡΑΦΙΚΑ ΕΙΔΗ (photographic items)
- and the main department stores:
  MARINOPOULOS
  MINION
  ATHENÈE
  TSITSOPOULOS
- The pavement kiosks (ΠΕΡΙΠΤΕΡΑ) are particularly useful as they are open late at night and sell a variety of goods such as aspirins, razor blades, playing cards, pens, soft drinks etc. See also 'The tobacconist's' p. 50 and 'Telephoning' p. 100.

WHAT TO SAY

Where can I buy ...?	Πού μπορῶ ν'ἀγοράσω ...;
	poo boro nag-ora-so ...
I'd like ...	Θά ἤθελα ...
	tha eethella ...
a bag	μία τσάντα
	mee-a tsanda
a beach ball	μία μπάλλα
	mee-a balla
a bucket	ἕνα κουβᾶ
	enna koova
an English newspaper	μία ἀγγλική ἐφημερίδα
	mee-a ang-leekee ef-eemehr-eetha
some envelopes	μερικούς φακέλους
	mehr-eek-ooss fak-el-ooss
a guide book	ἕνα βιβλίο ὁδηγό
	enna veev-lee-o othee-go
a map (of the area)	ἕνα χάρτη (τῆς περιοχῆς)
	enna hartee (teess peri-oheess)
some postcards	μερικές κάρτες
	mehr-eek-ess kartess

a spade	ἕνα φτυάρι
	enna ftee-*ar*-ee
a straw hat	ἕνα ψάθινο καπέλλο
	enna psathee-no kapell*o*
a suitcase	μία βαλίτσα
	mee-a valeet-sa
some sunglasses	γυαλιά ἡλίου
	yal-ya eelee-oo
a sunshade	μία τέντα ἡλίου
	mee-a tenda eelee-oo
an umbrella	μία ὀμπρέλλα
	mee-a ombrella
some writing paper	χαρτί ἀλληλογραφίας
	hartee alleel-ograf-*ee*-ass
I'd like . . . [*show the camera*]	Θά ἤθελα . . .
	tha *ee*thella . . .
a colour film	ἕνα ἔγχρωμο φίλμ
	enna en-hrom-o film
a black and white film	ἕνα ἀσπρόμαυρο φίλμ
	enna assprom-avro film
for prints	γιά φωτογραφίες
	ya fotograf-*ee*-ess
for slides	γιά σλάϊτς
	ya slides
12(24/36) exposures	γιά δώδεκα (εἴκοσι-τέσσερεσ/ τριάντα-ἕξη) φωτογραφίες
	ya thothe-ka (eekossee tesser-ess/ tree-anda eksee) fotograf-*ee*-ess
a standard 8 mm film	ἕνα κανονικό φίλμ τῶν ὀκτώ μιλιμέτρ
	enna kan-on-eeko-o film ton okt*o* millimetr
a super 8 film	ἕνα φίλμ σοῦπερ ὀκτώ
	enna film s*oo*per okt*o*
some flash bulbs	μερικά φλάς
	mehr-eeka flass
This camera is broken	Αὐτή ἡ φωτογραφική μηχανή χάλασε
	aftee ee fotografeekee meehanee halass-eh
The film is stuck	Τό φίλμ ἔχει μπλεχτεῖ
	toh film ehee bleh-ht*ee*

Please can you . . .	**Παρακαλῶ μπορεῖτε νά . . .**
	parakal*o* boreeteh na . . .
develop/print this?	ἐμφανίσετε/ἐκτυπώσετε αὐτό;
	emfan-*ee*sset-eh/ek-teeposset-eh afto
load the camera for me?	βάλετε τό φίλμ μέσα;
	valet-eh toh film messa

[For other essential expressions, see 'Shop talk', p. 58]

The tobacconist's

ESSENTIAL INFORMATION

- Tobacco is sold mainly in pavement kiosks called ΠΕΡΙΠΤΕΡΑ.
- To ask if there is one nearby, see p. 22.
- Kiosks always sell newspapers (Greek and foreign), sweets and sometimes postage stamps. See also p. 48 and p. 100.

WHAT TO SAY

A packet of cigarettes . . .	Ἕνα πακέτο τσιγάρα . . .
	enna pak-*et*-o tseegara . . .
with filters	μέ φίλτρο
	meh f*ee*ltro
without filters	χωρίς φίλτρο
	hor*ee*ss f*ee*ltro
menthol	μέντας
	men-tass
Those up there . . .	Ἐκεῖνα ἐκεῖ πάνω . . .
	ek-*ee*na ek-*ee* pan-o . . .
on the right	δεξιά
	theks-y*a*
on the left	ἀριστερά
	areesteh-r*a*
These [*point*]	Αὐτά
	aft*a*
Cigarettes, please . . .	Τσιγάρα, παρακαλῶ . . .
	tseegara parakal*o* . . .
100, 200, 300	ἑκατό, διακόσια, τριακόσια
	ek-at-*o*, thee-akoss-ya, tree-akoss-ya

Two packets	δύο πακέτα
	th*ee*-o pak-*et*-**a**
Have you got . . .	Ἔχετε . . .
	*e*h-het-eh . . .
English cigarettes?	ἐγγλέζικα τσιγάρα;
	engl*ez*-eeka tseeg*a*ra
American cigarettes?	ἀμερικάνικα τσιγάρα;
	amerikan-eeka tseeg*a*ra
English pipe tobacco?	ἐγγλέζικο καπνό γιά πίπα;
	engl*ez*-eeko kapn-*o* ya p*ee*pa
American pipe tobacco?	ἀμερικάνικο καπνό γιά πίπα;
	amerikan-eek-*o* kapn*o* ya p*ee*pa
A packet of pipe tobacco	Ἕνα πακέτο μέ καπνό πίπας
	*e*nna paket-o meh kapn*o* peep-ass
That one up there . . .	Ἐκεῖνο ἐκεῖ πάνω . . .
	ek-*ee*no ek-*ee* pan-o . . .
on the right	δεξιά
	theks-y*a*
on the left	ἀριστερά
	areesteh-r*a*
This one [*point*]	Αὐτό
	aft*o*
A cigar, please	Ἕνα πούρο, παρακαλῶ
	*e*nna p*oo*-ro parakal*o*
(Some) cigars	Πούρα
	p*oo*-ra
Those [*point*]	Ἐκεῖνα
	ek-*ee*na
A box of matches	Σπίρτα
	sp*ee*rta
A packet of pipe cleaners	Ἕνα πακέτο μέ καθαριστές πίπας
	*e*nna pak-et-o meh kathar-eestess peep-ass
A packet of flints	Ἕνα πακέτο μέ πέτρες
[*Show lighter*]	*e*nna pak-et-o meh petress
Lighter fuel	Βενζίνη γιά ἀναπτῆρα παρακαλῶ
	venz*ee*nee ya anapt*ee*ra parakal*o*
Lighter gas, please	Ἀέριο γιά ἀναπτῆρα
	a-*e*hrio ya anapt*ee*ra

[*For other essential expressions, see 'Shop talk', p. 58)*

Buying clothes

ESSENTIAL INFORMATION

- Look for:
  ΓΥΝΑΙΚΕΙΑ ΕΝΔΥΜΑΤΑ (women's clothes)
  ΑΝΔΡΙΚΑ ΕΝΔΥΜΑΤΑ (men's clothes)
  ΥΠΟΔΗΜΑΤΟΠΟΙΕΙΟΝ (shoe shop)
- Don't buy without being measured first or without trying things on.
- Don't rely on conversion charts of clothing sizes (see p. 139).
- If you are buying for someone else, take their measurements with you.

WHAT TO SAY

I'd like ...	Θά ἤθελα ...
	tha *ee*thella ...
an anorak	ἕνα ἀνοράκ
	*enn*a anor*ak*
a belt	μία ζώνη
	mee-a zon-ee
a bikini	ἕνα μπικίνι
	*enn*a bikini
a bra	ἕνα σουτιέν
	*enn*a sootyen
a cap (swimming, skiing)	ἕνα σκοῦφο (γιά τή θάλασσα/γιά σκί)
	*enn*a sk*oo*fo (ya tee th*a*l-assa/ya sk*ee*)
a cardigan	μία ζακέτα
	mee-a zak-*et*-a
a coat	ἕνα παλτό
	*enn*a palto
a dress	ἕνα φόρεμα
	*enn*a for-ema
a hat	ἕνα καπέλλο
	*enn*a kapello
a jacket	Ἕνα σακκάκι
	*enn*a sakk*ak*-ee
a jumper	μία μπλούζα
	mee-a bl*oo*za

a nightdress	ἕνα νυχτικό
	enna nee-hteeko
a pullover	ἕνα πουλόβερ
	enna pool-ovehr
a raincoat	ἕνα ἀδιάβροχο
	enna athee-avro-ho
a shirt	ἕνα πουκάμισο
	enna pookam-eeso
a skirt	μία φοῦστα
	mee-a foosta
a suit	ἕνα κοστούμι
	enna kostoomee
a swimsuit	ἕνα μαγιό
	enna ma-yo
a T-shirt	ἕνα μπλουζάκι
	enna bloozak-ee
I'd like a pair of . . .	Θά ἤθελα . . .
	tha eethella . . .
briefs (women)	μία κυλλότα
	mee-a keelot-a
gloves	γάντια
	gandia
jeans	ἕνα μπλού-τζήν
	enna blue-jean
pyjamas	μία πυτζάμα
	mee-a peetza-ma
shorts	ἕνα σόρτ
	enna sort
socks	κάλτσες ἀνδρικές
	kalt-sess andreek-ess
stockings	κάλτσες γυναικείες
	kalt-sess gheenek-ee-ess
tights	ἕνα καλσόν
	enna kalson
trousers	ἕνα πανταλόνι
	enna pantal-on-ee
underpants (men)	ἕνα σλίπ
	enna slip
I'd like a pair of . . .	Θά ἤθελα . . .
	tha eethella . . .
shoes	παπούτσια
	papootsia
canvas shoes	ἐλβιέλες
	elvee-el-ess

I'd like a pair of . . .	Θά ἤθελα . . .
	tha eethella . . .
sandals	πέδιλα
	peth-eela
beach shoes	σανδάλια
	san-thal-ya
smart shoes	βραδυνά παπούτσια
	vrathee-na papoots-ia
boots	μπότες
	bot-ess
moccasins	μοκασίνια
	mokas-eenya
My size is . . .	Τό νούμερο μου εἶναι . . .
[For numbers, see p. 125]	toh noomero moo eeneh
Can you measure me, please?	Μπορεῖτε νά μοῦ πάρετε τά μέτρα,
	παρακαλῶ;
	boreeteh na moo par-et-eh ta metra
	parakalo
Can I try it on?	Μπορῶ νά τό δοκιμάσω;
	boro na toh thok-eema-so
It's for a present	Εἶναι γιά δῶρο
	eeneh ya thoro
These are the measurements	Αὐτά εἶναι τά μέτρα
[show written]	afta eeneh ta metra
bust	στῆθος
	steethoss
chest	στῆθος
	steeth-oss
collar	κολλάρο
	kollar-o
hip	περιφέρεια
	peri-fehria
leg	πόδι
	poth-ee
waist	μέση
	messee
Have you got something . . .	Ἔχετε κάτι . . .
	eh-het-eh kat-ee . . .
in black?	σέ μαῦρο;
	seh mavro
in white?	σέ ἄσπρο;
	seh aspro

in grey?	σέ γκρί; seh gr*ee*
in blue?	σέ μπλέ; seh bleh
in brown?	σέ καφέ; seh ka*feh*
in pink?	σέ ρόζ; seh roz
in green?	σέ πράσινο; seh pr*as*-eeno
in red?	σέ κόκκινο; seh kok-eeno
in yellow?	σέ κίτρινο; seh k*ee*treeno
in this colour? [*point*]	σέ αὐτό τό χρῶμα; seh af*to* toh hroma
in cotton?	σέ βαμβακερό; seh vamvak-e*hro*
in denim?	σέ τραχύ ὕφασμα; seh trah*ee ee*fazma
in leather?	σέ δέρμα; seh th*ehr*-ma
in nylon?	σέ νάϋλον; seh n*a*-eelon
in suede?	σέ σουέτ; seh soo-*et*
in wool?	σέ μάλλινο; seh m*a*lleeno
in this material? [*point*]	σέ αὐτό τό ὕφασμα; seh af*to* toh *ee*fazma

[*For other essential expressions, see 'Shop talk', p. 58*]

Replacing equipment

ESSENTIAL INFORMATION

- Look for these shops and signs:
  ΣΙΔΗΡΟΠΩΛΕΙΟΝ (hardware)
  ΗΛΕΚΤΡΙΚΑ ΕΙΔΗ (electrical goods)
  ΨΙΛΙΚΑ (household cleaning material)
- To ask the way to the shop, see p. 22.
- At a campsite try their shop first.

WHAT TO SAY

Have you got . . .	Ἔχετε . . .
	eh-het-eh . . .
an adaptor? [show appliance]	ἕνα μετασχηματιστή;
	enna met-ass-heema-teest-ee
a bottle of butane gas?	ἕνα μπουκάλι γκάζι;
	enna bookalee gazee
a bottle opener?	ἀνοικτήρι γιά μπουκάλια;
	an-eekteeree ya bookalya
a corkscrew?	ἀνοικτήρι φιάλης;
	an-eekteeree fee-al-eess
any disinfectant?	ἕνα ἀπολυμαντικό;
	enna apol-eemandeeko
any disposable cups?	χάρτινα φλυτζάνια;
	harteena fleet-zan-ya
any disposable plates?	χάρτινα πιάτα;
	harteena pee-at-a
a drying up cloth?	πανί γιά τά πιάτα;
	pan-ee ya ta pee-at-a
any forks?	πηρούνια;
	peeroonia
a fuse? [show old one]	ἀσφάλεια;
	asfal-ya
an insecticide spray?	ἕνα ἐντομοκτόνο;
	enna endomokton-o
a paper kitchen roll?	ἕνα ρολό γιά κουζίνα (χαρτί);
	enna rolo ya koozeena (hartee)
any knives?	μαχαίρια;
	ma-hehrya

a light bulb? [*show old one*]	μία λάμπα; mee-a lamba
a plastic bucket?	ένα πλαστικό κουβᾶ; enna plasteeko koova
a plastic can?	ένα πλαστικό δοχείο; enna plasteeko tho-hee-o
a scouring pad?	ένα σῦρμα γιά πιάτα; enna seerma ha pee-at-a
a spanner?	ένα κλειδί; enna kleeth-ee
a sponge?	ένα σφουγγάρι; enna sfoongar-ee
any string?	σπάγγο; spango
any tent pegs?	πάσσαλους σκηνῆς; passal-ooss skeen-eess
a tin opener?	ένα ἀνοικτήρι γιά κονσέρβες; enna an-eekteeree ya kon-sehr-vess
a torch?	ένα φάκο; enna fak-o
any torch batteries?	μπαταρίες γιά φακούς; batar-ee-ess ya fak-ooss
a universal plug (for the sink)?	ένα βούλωμα (γιά τό νεροχύτη); enna vooloma (ya toh nehro-heetee)
a washing line?	σκοινί γιά τό στέγνωμα τῶν ρούχων; skeenee ya toh stegnoma ton roo-hon
any washing powder?	σκόνη γιά πλύσιμο; skon-ee ya pleess-eemo
any washing up liquid?	ὑγρό γιά τά πιάτα; eegro ya ta pee-at-a
a washing-up brush?	βούρτσα γιά τά πιάτα; voortsa ya ta pee-at-a

[*For other essential expressions, see 'Shop talk', p. 58*]

Shop talk

ESSENTIAL INFORMATION

- Know your coins and notes
  coins: see illustration
  notes: 50 drachmas, 100 drachmas, 500 drachmas, 1,000 drachmas
- Know how to say the important weights and measures:

50 grams	πενήντα γραμμάρια
	pen-*eenda* gramm*a*-ria
100 grams	ἑκατό γραμμάρια
	ek-at-*o* gramm*a*-ria
200 grams	διακόσια γραμμάρια
	thee-ak*oss*-ya gramm*a*-ria
½ kilo	μισό κιλό
	mees*so* keel*o*
1 kilo	ἕνα κιλό
	enna keel*o*
2 kilos	δύο κιλά
	th*ee*-o keel*a*
½ litre	μισό λίτρο
	mees*so* leetro
1 litre	ἕνα λίτρο
	enna leetro
2 litres	δύο λίτρα
	th*ee*-o leetra

[For numbers, see p. 125]

- There are sales in January and August when many shops give discounts of 10% on all goods.
- Bargaining is less and less common but if you feel you are being overcharged – particularly for tourist items – try suggesting a more reasonable price.
- In small shops don't be surprised, if customers, as well as the shop assistant, say 'hello' and 'goodbye' to you.

CUSTOMER

Hello	Γειά σας
	yassas
Good morning ⎤	Καλημέρα
Good day ⎦	kal-eemehra
Good afternoon (after siesta) ⎤	Καλησπέρα
Good evening ⎦	kal-eespehra
Goodbye	Γειά σας
	yassas
I'm just looking	Ρίχνω μιά ματιά
	reehno mee-a mat-ya
Excuse me	Μέ συγχωρεῖτε
	meh seen-horeet-eh
How much is this/that?	Πόσο κάνει αὐτό/ἐκεῖνο;
	posso kan-ee afto/ek-eeno
What is that?	Τί εἶναι ἐκεῖνο;
	tee eeneh ek-eeno
What are those?	Τί εἶναι ἐκεῖνα;
	tee eeneh ek-eena
Is there a discount?	Κάνετε ἔκπτωση;
	kan-et-eh ekptoss-ee
I'd like that, please	Θά ἤθελα ἐκεῖνο, παρακαλῶ
	tha eethalla ek-eeno parakalo
Not that	Ὄχι ἐκεῖνο
	o-hee ek-eeno
Like that	Σάν ἐκεῖνο
	san ek-eeno
That's enough, thank you	Φτάνει, εὐχαριστῶ
	ftan-ee ef-har-eesto
More, please	Περισσότερο, παρακαλῶ
	perissot-ehro parakalo
Less than that, please	Λιγότερο ἀπό αὐτό, παρακαλῶ
	leegot-ehro apo afto parakalo
That's fine ⎤	Ἐντάξει
OK ⎦	endaksee
I won't take it, thank you	Δέν θά τό πάρω, εὐχαριστῶ
	then tha toh par-o ef-har-eesto
It's not right	Δέν εἶναι σωστό
	then eeneh sosto
Thank you very much	Εὐχαριστῶ πάρα πολύ
	ef-har-eesto para pol-ee

Have you got something . . .	Ἔχετε κάτι . . .
	eh-het-eh kat-ee . . .
better?	καλύτερο;
	kal-eet-ehro
cheaper?	φθηνότερο;
	ftheenot-ehro
different?	διαφορετικό;
	thee-afor-et-eeko
larger?	μεγαλύτερο;
	meg-aleet-ehro
smaller?	μικρότερο;
	meekrot-ehro
At what time do you . . .	Τί ὥρα . . .
	tee ora . . .
open?	ἀνοίγετε;
	aneeget-eh
close?	κλείνετε;
	kleenet-eh
Can I have a bag, please?	Μπορῶ νά ἔχω μία τσάντα,
	παρακαλῶ;
	boro na eh-ho mee-a tsanda
	parakalo
Can I have a receipt?	Μπορῶ νά ἔχω μία ἀπόδειξη;
	boro na eh-ho mee-a apoth-eeksee
Do you take . . .	Παίρνετε . . .
	pehr-net-eh . . .
English/American money?	ἐγγλέζικα/ἀμερικάνικα λεφτά;
	englez-eeka/amerikan-eeka lefta
travellers cheques?	τράβελερς τσέκς;
	travellers' cheques
credit cards?	πιστωτικές κάρτες;
	peestohteekess kartess
I'd like that . . .	Θά ἤθελα . . .
	tha eethella . . .
one like that	ἕνα σάν ἐκεῖνο
	enna san ek-eeno
two like that	δύο σάν ἐκεῖνο
	theeo san ek-eeno

SHOP ASSISTANT

Can I help you?	Μπορῶ νά σᾶς βοηθήσω;
	boro na sas vo-eeth-*ee*sso
What would you like?	Τί θά θέλατε;
	tee tha thellat-eh
Will that be all?⎤	Τίποτα ἄλλο;
Is that all?	teepota *a*llo
Anything else? ⎦	
Would you like it wrapped?	Θέλετε νά σᾶς τό τυλίξω;
	thellet-eh na sas toh teeleek-so
Sorry, none left	Λυπᾶμαι, δέν ἔχει μείνει
	τίποτα
	.leepam-eh then eh-hee meenee
	teepota
I haven't got any	Δέν ἔχω
	then eh-ho
I haven't got any more	Δέν μοῦ ἔχει μείνει τίποτα
	then moo eh-hee meenee teepota
How many do you want?⎤	Πόσα θέλετε;
How much do you want?⎦	possa thellet-eh
Is that enough?	Φτάνει αὐτό;
	ftan-ee afto

Shopping for food

Bread

ESSENTIAL INFORMATION

- Finding a baker's, see p. 22.
- Key words to look for:
  ΑΡΤΟΠΟΙΕΙΟΝ (baker's)
  ΨΩΜΙ (bread)
- Some supermarkets sell bread.
- Bakers are generally open between 7.30 a.m. to 8.30 p.m.
- All loaves are sold by weight, rolls by item.

WHAT TO SAY

Some bread, please	Ψωμί, παρακαλῶ psom-*ee* parakalo
A loaf (like that)	Ἕνα ψωμί (σάν ἐκείνο) enna psom-*ee* (san ek-*een*-o)
A large one	Ἕνα μεγάλο ψωμί enna megalo psom-*ee*
A small one	Ἕνα μικρό ψωμί enna meekro psom-*ee*
A bread roll	Ἕνα ψωμάκι enna psomak-ee
Four bread rolls	Τέσσερα ψωμάκια tessera psomak-ya
Two French-type loaves	Δύο φραντζόλες th*ee*-o frant-zol-ess
½ kilo of white bread	Μισό κιλό ἄσπρο ψωμί meesso keelo aspro psom-*ee*
1 kilo of brown bread	Ἕνα κιλό ψωμί μαῦρο enna keelo psom-*ee* mavr-o

[*For other essential expressions, see 'Shop talk', p. 58*]

Cakes

ESSENTIAL INFORMATION

- Key words to look for:
  ΖΑΧΑΡΟΠΛΑΣΤΕΙΟΝ (a place to buy cakes and have a drink)
  ΓΑΛΑΚΤΟΠΩΛΕΙΟΝ (milk bars specializing in dairy produce,
  e.g. rice puddings, yoghurt, ice-creams etc., but which also serve
  cakes. See p. 79 for 'Ordering a drink'.)
- To find a cake shop, see p. 22.

WHAT TO SAY

The types of cake you find in the shops vary from region to region
but the following are some of the most common.

μπακλαβᾶ baklava	mille feuilles pastry with nuts and honey
καταΐφι kata-*ee*fee	fine shredded pastry with walnuts and honey
γαλακτομπούρεκο galakto-b*oo*rek-o	semolina
λουκουμάδες lookoom*ath*-ess	small doughnuts fried in oil and served with honey
σοκολατίνα sokolat*ee*na	chocolate cake
πάστα ἀμυγδάλου p*a*sta ameegth*al*-oo	almond cake
μπουγάτσα boog*a*tsa	flaky pastry filled with custard
ριζόγαλο reez*o*galo	rice pudding
γιαούρτι ya-*oo*rtee	yoghurt

You usually buy medium sized cakes by item:

Two éclairs, please	Δύο ἐκλαίρ, παρακαλῶ th*ee*-o eclair parakal*o*

You buy small cakes by weight:

200 grams of petits fours	Διακόσια γραμμάρια κουλούρια, παρακαλῶ thee-akoss-ya gramma-ria kooloo-ria
400 grams of biscuits	Τετρακόσια γραμμάρια μπισκότα tetra-koss-ya gramma-ria beeskota

You may also want to say:

A selection, please	Διάφορα γλυκά, παρακαλῶ thee-af-ora gleeka parakalo

[*For other essential expressions, see 'Shop talk', p. 58*]

Ice-cream and sweets

ESSENTIAL INFORMATION

- Key words to look for:
  ΠΑΓΩΤΑ (ice-cream)
  ΖΑΧΑΡΟΠΛΑΣΤΕΙΟΝ (cake shop)
  ΖΑΧΑΡΟΠΛΑΣΤΗΣ (cake/pastry maker)
- Best-known ice-cream brand names:
  ΕΒΓΑ
  ΔΕΛΤΑ
- Prepacked sweets are available in general stores, supermarkets and kiosks.
- Kiosks often have small fridges with ice-creams.

WHAT TO SAY

A . . . ice, please	Ἕνα παγωτό . . . παρακαλῶ
	enna pago*to* . . . parakal*o*
vanilla	βανίλα
	van*i*lla
chocolate	σοκολάτα
	sokol*a*-ta
cream	κρέμα
	krem-a
cassata	κασσάτο
	kass*a*t-o
lemon	λεμόνι
	lemon-ee
strawberry	φράουλα
	fra-oola
cherry	βύσσινο
	veessino
Two . . . ices [*specify flavour as above*]	Δύο παγωτά . . .
	thee-o pagota . . .
A double	Ἕνα διπλό παγωτό
	enna theepl*o* pago*to*
Two doubles	Δύο διπλά παγωτά
	thee-o theepl*a* pago*ta*

A cone	Ένα παγωτό χωνάκι
	enna pagoto honak-ee
A wafer	Ένα σάντουϊτς
	enna sandwich
A tub	Ένα κύπελλο
	enna keepello
A lollipop	Ένα γλυφιτζούρι
	enna glee-feet-zooree
A packet of ...	Ένα πακέτο ....
	enna pak-et-o ...
chewing gum	τσίχλες
	tseehles
sweets	καραμέλες
	karamel-ess
toffees	ζαχαρωτά
	za-harota
chocolates	σοκολατάκια
	sokolatak-ya
mints	μέντες
	men-tess

[*For other essential expressions, see 'Shop talk', p. 58*]

In the supermarket

ESSENTIAL INFORMATION

- The place to ask for: [see p. 22]
  ΣΟΥΠΕΡΜΑΡΚΕΤ (supermarket)
  ΠΑΝΤΟΠΩΛΕΙΟΝ (grocer's)
- Key instructions on signs in the shop:
  ΕΙΣΟΔΟΣ (entrance)
  ΕΞΟΔΟΣ (exit)
  ΑΠΑΓΟΡΕΥΕΤΑΙ Η ΕΙΣΟΔΟΣ (no entry)
  ΤΑΜΕΙΟΝ (cash desk)
  ΕΙΔΙΚΗ ΠΡΟΣΦΟΡΑ (special offer)
  ΣΕΛΦ–ΣΕΡΒΙΣ (self-service)
- Opening times vary but are generally 8.00 a.m. to 2.00 p.m. and 5.00 p.m. to 8.00 p.m.
- For non-food items, see 'Replacing equipment', p. 56.
- No need to say anything in a supermarket, but ask if you can't see what you want.

WHAT TO SAY

Excuse me, please	Μέ συγχωρεῖτε, παρακαλῶ
	meh seenhor*ee*teh parakal*o*
Where is . . .	Πού εἶναι . . .
	p*oo* *ee*neh . . .
the bread?	τό ψωμί;
	toh psom-*ee*
the butter?	τό βούτυρο;
	toh v*oo*teero
the cheese?	τό τυρί;
	toh teer*ee*
the chocolate?	ἡ σοκολάτα;
	ee sokol*a*-ta
the coffee?	ὁ καφές;
	o kaf-*ess*
the cooking oil?	τό λάδι γιά μαγείρεμα;
	toh lath-ee ya mag-*ee*rema
the fish?	τά ψάρια;
	toh ps*ar*-eea

the fruit?	τά φρούτα;
	ta froota
the honey?	τό μέλι;
	toh mel-ee
the jam?	οἱ μαρμελάδες;
	ee marmel-athess
the meat?	τό κρέας;
	toh kreh-ass
the milk?	τό γάλα;
	toh ga-la
the mineral water?	τό ἐμφιαλωμένο νερό;
	toh emfee-alomen-o nehro
the salt?	τό ἀλάτι;
	toh alat-ee
the sugar?	ἡ ζάχαρη;
	ee za-har-ee
the tea?	τό τσάι;
	toh tsa-ee
the tinned fish?	οἱ κονσέρβες μέ ψάρια;
	ee konsehr-vess meh psaria
the tinned fruit?	οἱ κονσέρβες μέ φρούτα;
	ee konsehr-vess meh froota
the vinegar?	τό ξύδι;
	toh ksee-thee
the wine?	τά κρασιά;
	ta krass-ya
the yoghurt?	τό γιαούρτι;
	toh ya-oortee
Where are . . .	Ποῦ εἶναι . . .
	poo eeneh . . .
the biscuits?	τά μπισκότα;
	ta bee-skota
the crisps?	τά πατατάκια;
	ta patatak-ia
the eggs?	τά αὐγά;
	ta avga
the frozen foods?	τά καταψυγμένα τρόφιμα;
	ta kataps-eegmenna trof-eema
the fruit juices?	οἱ χυμοί φρούτων;
	ee heemee frooton
the pastas?	τά ζυμαρικά;
	ta zeemar-eeka

Where are . . .	Ποῦ εἶναι . . .
	poo eeneh . . .
the seafoods?	τά θαλασσινά;
	ta thalasseena
the snails?	τά σαλιγκάρια;
	ta saleengar-eea
the soft drinks?	τά ἀναψυκτικά ποτά;
	ta anaps-eek-teeka pota
the sweets?	οἱ καραμέλες;
	ee karamel-ess
the tinned vegetables?	οἱ κονσέρβες μέ λαχανικά;
	ee konsehr-vess meh la-han-eeka
the vegetables?	τά λαχανικά;
	ta la-han-eeka

[*For other essential expressions, see 'Shop talk', p. 58*]

Picnic food

ESSENTIAL INFORMATION

- Key words to look for:
  ΠΑΝΤΟΠΩΛΕΙΟΝ (grocer's)
  ΣΟΥΠΕΡΜΑΡΚΕΤ (supermarket)
  ΣΕ ΠΑΚΕΤΟ (take-away)
- Hot food to take away can be bought in restaurants and pizza houses.
- Weight guide: 4–6 oz/150 g of prepared salad per two people, if eaten as a starter to substantial meal. 3–4 oz/100 g of prepared salad per person, if to be eaten as the main part of a picnic-type meal.

WHAT TO SAY

A slice of . . .	Μία φέτα . . .
	mee-a fet-a . . .
Two slices of . . .	Δύο φέτες . . .
	thee-o fet-ess . . .
ham	ζαμπόν
	zambon

garlic sausage	λουκάνικο μέ σκόρδο
	lookan-eeko meh skortho
salami	σαλάμι
	salam-ee
mortadella	μορταδέλλα
	mortathella
100 grams of ...	Ἑκατό γραμμάρια ...
	ek-ato gramma–ria ...
150 grams of ...	Ἑκατό πενῆντα γραμμάρια ...
	ek-ato pen-eenda gramma-ria ...
200 grams of ...	Διακόσια γραμμάρια ...
	thee-akoss-ya gramma-ria ...
300 grams of ...	Τριακόσια γραμμάρια ...
	tree-akoss-ya gramma-ria ...
Russian salad	ρωσική σαλάτα
	rosseekee sala-ta
olives (black/green)	ἐλιές (μαῦρες/πράσινες)
	el-ee-ess (mavr-ess/prasseen-ess)
cheese	τυρί
	teeree

You may also like to try some of these:

ταραμοσαλάτα	cod's roe mixed with oil and lemon
taramo-sala-ta	
φέτα	white cheese made of goat's milk
fet-a	
κασέρι	yellow cheese, rich in cream
kassehr-ee	
κεφαλοτύρι	very salty yellow cheese
kef-aloteer-ee	
μανούρι	very creamy white cheese
manooree	
μυτζήθρα	white soft cheese made from ewe's
meetzeethra	milk
χαλβάς	sweet made from sesame seeds or
halv-ass	semolina, and honey

[For other essential expressions see 'shoptalk', p. 58]

Fruit and vegetables

ESSENTIAL INFORMATION

- Key words to look for:
  ΦΡΟΥΤΑ (fruit)
  ΟΠΟΡΟΠΩΛΕΙΟΝ (greengrocer's)
  ΛΑΧΑΝΙΚΑ (vegetables)
- If possible buy fruit and vegetables in the market where they are cheaper and fresher than in the shops. Open air markets are held once or twice a week in most areas, usually in the mornings.
- It is customary for you to choose your own fruit and vegetables at the market and for the stallholder to weigh and price them. You must take your own shopping bag – paper and plastic bags are not normally provided.
- Weight guide: 1 kilo of potatoes is sufficient for six people for one meal.

WHAT TO SAY

½ kilo of . . .	Μισό κιλό . . .
	meess*o* keel*o* . . .
1 kilo of . . .	Ἕνα κιλό . . .
	*e*nna keel*o* . . .
2 kilos of . . .	Δύο κιλά . . .
	th*ee*-o keel*a* . . .
apples	μῆλα
	m*ee*la
apricots	βερύκοκκα
	vehr-*ee*koka
bananas	μπανάνες
	banan-ess
cherries	κεράσια
	kehr-*ass*-ya
figs	σῦκα
	s*ee*ka
grapes (white/black)	σταφύλια (ἄσπρα/μαῦρα)
	staf-*eel*-ya (*a*spra/m*a*vra)
oranges	πορτοκάλια
	portokal-ya

peaches	ροδάκινα
	rothak-eena
pears	ἀχλάδια
	a-hlath-ya
plums	δαμάσκηνα
	thamask-eena
strawberries	φράουλες
	fra-ool-ess
A pineapple, please	Ἕναν ἀνανᾶ, παρακαλῶ
	ennan anana parakalo
A grapefruit	Μία φράπα
	mee-a frap-a
A melon/water melon	Ἕνα πεπόνι/καρπούζι
	enna pep-on-ee/karpoozee
250 grams of . . .	Διακόσια-πενῆντα γραμμάρια . . .
	thee-a-koss-ya pen-eenda gramma-ria . . .
½ kilo of . . .	Μισό κιλό . . .
	meesso keelo . . .
1 kilo of . . .	Ἕνα κιλό . . .
	enna keelo . . .
1½ kilos of . . .	Ἕνάμισο κιλό . . .
	enna-meesso keelo . . .
2 kilos of . . .	Δύο κιλά . . .
	thee-o keela . . .
aubergines	μελιτζάνες
	mel-eetzan-ess
beetroot	παντζάρια
	pannzar-eea
carrots	καροττα
	karota
courgettes	κολοκυθάκια
	kolokee-thak-ya
green beans	φασολάκια
	fassolak-ya
leeks	πράσσα
	prassa
mushrooms	μανιτάρια
	maneeta-ria
onions	κρεμμύδια
	kremmeeth-ya

2 kilos of . . .	Δύο κιλά . . .
	th*ee*-o k*ee*la . . .
peas	μπιζέλια
	beezel-ya
peppers (green/red)	πιπεριές (πράσινες/κόκκινες)
	pee-peh-ree-*ess* (pr*a*sseen-ess/
	k*o*keen-ess)
potatoes	πατάτες
	pat*a*t-ess
spinach	σπανάκι
	span*a*k-ee
tomatoes	ντομάτες
	dom*a*t-ess
A bunch of . . .	Ἕνα ματσάκι . . .
	*e*nna mats*a*k-ee . . .
parsley	μαϊντανό
	may-dan-*o*
radishes	ραπανάκια
	rapan*a*k-ya
A head of garlic	Ἕνα σκόρδο
	*e*nna sk*o*rtho
A lettuce	Ἕνα μαρούλι
	*e*nna mar*oo*lee
A cauliflower	Ἕνα κουνουπίδι
	*e*nna koonoop*ee*thee
A cabbage	Ἕνα λάχανο
	*e*nna l*a*-hano
A cucumber	Ἕνα ἀγγούρι
	*e*nna ang*oo*ree
Like that, please	Ὅπως ἐκεῖνο, παρακαλῶ
	*o*p-oss ek-*ee*no parakal*o*

These are some fruit and vegetables with which you may not be familiar:

μούσμουλα	medlars: small slightly sour fruit,
m*oo*smoola	orange colour, juicy, eaten raw.
κυδώνι	quince: pale yellow apple-shaped
keethon-ee	fruit, sharp, mostly served with
	sugar
μπάμιες	okra: also called 'ladies' fingers'
bam-yess	

[*For other essential expressions, see 'Shop talk', p. 58*]

Meat

ESSENTIAL INFORMATION

- Key words to look for:
  ΚΡΕΟΠΩΛΕΙΟΝ (butcher's)
  ΚΡΕΟΠΩΛΗΣ (butcher)
- Weight guide: 4–6 oz/125–200 g of meat per person for one meal.
- There are no labels on counters and supermarket displays in Greece which could help you in deciding what cut or joint to have, so you will have to ask or simply point. Do not expect, however, to find the same cuts of meat as at your butcher at home.
- Pork in Greece is of a very high quality.

WHAT TO SAY

For a joint, choose the type of meat and then say how many people it is for:

Some beef, please	Βοδινό, παρακαλῶ
	vothee-no parakalo
Some lamb	Ἀρνάκι
	arnak-ee
Some pork	Χοιρινό
	heereeno
Some veal	Μοσχαρίσιο
	moss-har-ees-yo
A joint . . .	Ἕνα κομμάτι . . .
	enna kommat-ee . . .
for two people	γιά δύο ἄτομα
	ya thee-o atoma
for four people	γιά τέσσερα ἄτομα
	ya tessera atoma
for six people	γιά ἕξη ἄτομα
	ya eksee atoma

For steak, liver or kidneys, do as above:

Some steak, please	Μπόν φιλέ, παρακαλῶ
	bon feeleh parakalo
Some liver	Συκωτάκια
	seekotak-ya

Some kidneys	Νεφρά nefra
Some sausages	Λούκάνικα lookan-eeka
Some mince . . .	Κιμά . . . keema . . .
for three people	γιά τρία άτομα ya tree-a atoma
for five people	γιά πέντε άτομα ya pendeh atoma

For chops do it this way:

Two veal escalopes, please	Δύο μοσχαρίσιες μπριζόλες,
	  παρακαλώ
	Thee-o moss-ha-rees-yess
	  breezol-ess parakalo

Three pork chops	Τρεῖς χοιρινές μπριζόλες treess heereen-ess breezol-ess
Five lamb chops	Πέντε ἀρνίσιες μπριζόλες pendeh arneess-yess breezol-ess

You may also want:

A chicken	Ἕνα κοτόπουλο enna kotop-oolo
A rabbit	Ἕνα κουνέλι enna koonel-ee
A tongue	Μία γλῶσσα mee-a glossa

Other essential expressions [see also p. 58]

Please can you . . .	Παρακαλώ μπορεῖτε νά . . . parakalo boreeteh na . . .
mince it?	τό κάνετε κιμά; toh kan-et-eh keema
dice it?	τό κόψετε; toh kopset-eh
trim the fat?	βγάλετε τό λῖπος; vgal-et-eh toh leeposs

Fish

ESSENTIAL INFORMATION

- The place to ask for: ΨΑΡΑΔΙΚΟ (fish shop)
- Another key word to look for is: ΘΑΛΑΣΣΙΝΑ (seafood)
- Markets usually have fresh fish stalls.
- Weight guide: 8 oz/250 g minimum per person for one meal of fish bought on the bone i.e.

½ kilo/500 g	for two people
1 kilo	for four people
1½ kilos	for six people

- You will find that cod and herring are sold dried and salted: they simply require soaking in water overnight.

WHAT TO SAY

Purchase most fish by weight:

½ kilo of . . .	Μισό κιλό . . .
	meesso keelo . . .
1 kilo of . . .	Ἕνα κιλό . . .
	enna keelo . . .
1½ kilos of . . .	Ἑνάμισο κιλό . . .
	enna-meesso keelo . . .
anchovies	ἀντσούγες
	ants-oog-ess
grey mullet	λυθρίνια
	lee-threen-eea
mussels	μύδια
	meeth-ya
octopus	χταπόδια
	htapoth-ya
oysters	στρείδια
	streeth-ya
prawns	γαρίδες
	ga-reethess
red mullet	μπαρμπούνια
	barboon-ya
sardines	σαρδέλες
	sar-thel-ess

smelt (fried)	μαρίδες (τιγανιτές)
	ma-reethess (teeganeetess)
squid	καλαμάρια
	kalama-ria
shrimps	γαρίδες
	ga-reethess
sea bream	συναγρίδες
	seen-agreeth-ess
trout	πέστροφες
	pestrof-ess
cod	μπακαλιάρο
	bakal-ya-ro

For some shellfish and 'frying pan' fish, specify the number:

A crab, please	Ἕνα καβούρι, 'παρακαλῶ
	enna kavoo-ree parakalo
A lobster	Ἕναν ἀστακό
	ennan astako
A trout	Μία πέστροφα
	mee-a pestrofa
A sole	Μία γλῶσσα
	mee-a glossa
A mackerel	Ἕνα σκουμπρί
	enna skoombree
A herring	Μία ρέγγα
	mee-a renga

Other essential expressions [see also p. 58]

Please can you . . .	Παρακαλῶ μπορεῖτε νά . . .
	parakalo boreeteh na . . .
take the heads off?	βγάλετε τά κεφάλια;
	vgal-et-eh ta kef-al-ya
clean them?	τά καθαρίσετε;
	ta katha-reeset-eh
fillet them?	βγάλετε τά κοκκάλα;
	vgal-et-eh ta kok-al-a

Eating and drinking out

Ordering a drink

ESSENTIAL INFORMATION

- The places to ask for: ΜΠΑΡ (bar), ΣΝΑΚ–ΜΠΑΡ (snack bar), ΟΥΖΕΡΙ (bar which serves hors d'oeuvres)
  ΖΑΧΑΡΟΠΛΑΣΤΕΙΟ (pastry shop which serves drinks as well)
  ΚΑΦΕΝΕΙΟ (coffee house, where Greek women are rarely seen)
- By law the price list (ΤΙΜΟΛΟΓΙΟΝ) must be on display. Service is usually included.
- Bars open late in the afternoon and close at 2.00 a.m. All other establishments are normally open all day.
- Bars and cafés serve both non-alcoholic and alcoholic drinks. Children are allowed in.
- Greek beer comes in small bottles of 350 g (about ½ pint) and 500 g (about 1 pint).
- Greek coffee is made by heating water, mixing in the ground coffee and sugar, and bringing it to the boil – it is very strong.

WHAT TO SAY

I'll have . . . please	Θέλω . . . παρακαλῶ
	thello . . . parakalo
a black coffee	ἕνα νέσκαφε σκέτο
	enna nescafe sket-o
a coffee with milk	ἕνα καφέ μέ γάλα
	enna kaf-eh meh ga-la
a Greek coffee	ἕνα Ἑλληνικό καφέ
	enna elleen-eeko kaf-eh
without sugar	σκέτο
	sket-o
medium sweet	μέτριο
	metrio
sweet	γλυκό
	gleeko
a tea	ἕνα τσάϊ
	enna tsa-ee
with milk	μέ γάλα
	meh ga-la
with lemon	μέ λεμόνι
	meh lem-on-ee

I'll have . . . please	Θέλω . . . παρακαλῶ
	thello . . . parakalo
a glass of milk	ἕνα ποτήρι γάλα
	enna poteeree ga-la
a hot chocolate	μία ζεστή σοκολάτα
	mee-a zestee sokola-ta
an iced coffee	ἕνα νέσκαφε φραπέ
	enna nescafe frap-eh
a mineral water	ἐμφιαλωμένο νερό
	emfee-alomen-o nehro
a lemonade	μία λεμονάδα
	mee-a lem-on-atha
a lemon squash	μία λεμονάδα χυμό
	mee-a lem-on-atha heemo
a Coca-Cola	μία κόκα κόλα
	mee-a koka kola
an orangeade	μία πορτοκαλάδα
	mee-a portokal-atha
an orange juice	μία πορτοκαλάδα χυμό
	mee-a portokal-atha heemo
a pineapple juice	ἕναν ἀνανᾶ χυμό
	ennan anana heemo
a beer	μία μπύρα
	mee-a bee-ra
a large bottle	ἕνα μεγάλο μπουκάλι
	enna megalo bookalee
a small bottle	ἕνα μικρό μπουκάλι
	enna meekro bookal-ee
A glass of . . .	Ἕνα ποτήρι . . .
	enna poteeree . . .
Two glasses of . . .	Δύο ποτήρια . . .
	thee-o poteeria . . .
A bottle of . . .	Ἕνα μπουκάλι . . .
	enna bookal-ee . . .
Two bottles of . . .	Δύο μπουκάλια . . .
	thee-o bookal-ya . . .
red wine	κόκκινο κρασί
	kokino krassee
white wine	ἄσπρο κρασί
	aspro krassee
rosé wine	ροζέ
	roz-eh

dry	ξυρό
	kseero
sweet	γλυκό
	gleeko
champagne	σαμπάνια
	sampan-ya
A whisky	Ἕνα οὐίσκι
	enna oo-eeskee
with ice	μέ πάγο
	meh pag-o
with water	μέ νερό
	meh nehro
with soda	μέ σόδα
	meh sotha
A gin	Ἕνα τζίν
	enna gin
with tonic	μέ τόνικ
	meh ton-ic
with lemon	μέ λεμόνι
	meh lem-on-ee
A brandy	Ἕνα κονιάκ
	enna konyak

These are local drinks you may like to try:

ρετσίνα ret-seena	a resinated wine (the resin added to the vats during fermentation gives this white wine its distinctive flavour)
μαυροδάφνη mavro-thafnee	a dessert wine (sweet and dark)
οὐζο oozo	an aniseed-flavoured aperitif
μαστίχα masteeeha	a sweet aperitif flavoured with mastic (the resin from the lentisk tree)
κουμκουάτ koom-koo-at	a liqueur made from tiny oranges: a speciality of Corfu
βυσσινάδα vees-seen-atha	a soft drink made from cherries

Other essential expressions:

Miss! [*This does not sound abrupt in Greek*]	Δεσποινίς! thespeen-*ee*ss
Waiter!	Γκαρσόν! garson
The bill, please	Τό λογαριασμό, παρακαλῶ toh logaree-azmo parakalo
How much does that come to?	Πόσο κάνει; posso kan-ee
Is service included?	Εἶναι μέ τό σερβίς; *ee*neh meh toh serv*ee*ss
Where is the toilet, please?	Ποῦ εἶναι ἡ τουαλέτα, παρακαλῶ; p*oo* *ee*neh ee too-al-et-a parakalo

Ordering a snack

ESSENTIAL INFORMATION

- Look for a café or small shop with any of the following signs:
  ΣΝΑΚ-ΜΠΑΡ (snack bar)
  ΟΥΖΕΡΙ (bar which serves hors d'oeuvres)
  ΚΑΦΕΝΕΙΟ (coffee house)
- Look for the names of snacks (listed below) on signs in the window
  or inside on the walls e.g.
  ΤΥΡΟΠΙΤΕΣ (cheese pies)
- For cakes, see p. 64.
- For ice-cream, see p. 66.
- For picnic-type snacks, see p. 70.
- For ordering a drink, see p. 79.

WHAT TO SAY

I'll have . . . please	Θέλω . . . παρακαλῶ
	thello . . . parakalo
a cheese sandwich	ἕνα σάντουϊτς μέ τυρί
	enna sandwich meh teeree
a ham sandwich	ἕνα σάντουϊτς μέ ζαμπόν
	enna sandwich meh zambon
a meat pie	μία κρεατόπιττα
	mee-a kreh-at-op-ita
a spinach pie	μία σπανακόπιττα
	meea-a spanak-op-ita
a cheese pie	μία τυρόπιττα
	mee-a teer-op-ita
a hot dog	ἕνα χότ ντόγκ
	enna hot dog

This is another snack you may like to try:

ἕνα σουβλάκι	pieces of grilled meat wrapped in a
enna soovlak-ee	type of pancake; doner kebab

In a restaurant

ESSENTIAL INFORMATION

- To find a restaurant, see p. 22.
- You can eat at the following places:
  ΕΣΤΙΑΤΟΡΙΟΝ (restaurant)
  ΤΑΒΕΡΝΑ (typical Greek restaurant)
  ΨΑΡΟΤΑΒΕΡΝΑ (restaurant specialising in seafood)
  ΨΗΣΤΑΡΙΑ (restaurant specialising in charcoal-grilled food)
- In smaller restaurants there may be no printed menu, so you will either have to ask what is available or look at the food displayed and point. The Greeks themselves often go into the kitchen to choose their meal.
- If the menu lists two prices for each item, the second price includes a 10% service charge, but an extra tip is always welcome.
- If there is a wine waiter (he will also serve the water and bread), a small tip should be left for him on the table (not on the plate with the bill).
- Times when restaurants stay open depend on the area and the season. However, they are normally open from midday to 4.00 p.m. and 8.00 p.m. to midnight. Although Greeks tend to eat late in the summer, all restaurants, bars and cafés are obliged by law to close at 2.00 a.m.
- In most tavernas and many restaurants draught wine is available. It is served in small cans and sold by weight. Order 1 kilo (1 litre), ½ kilo (½ litre) or ¼ kilo (a large glass).

WHAT TO SAY

May I book a table?	Μπορῶ νά κλείσω ἕνα τραπέζι;
	boro na kléeso enna trap-ez-ee
I've booked a table	Ἔχω κλείσει τραπέζι
	eh-ho kleessee trap-ez-ee
A table . . .	Ἕνα τραπέζι . . .
	enna trap-ez-ee . . .
for one	γιά ἕναν
	ya ennan
for three	γιά τρεῖς
	ya treess

The menu, please	Τόν κατάλογο παρακαλῶ
	ton kat*a*logo parakal*o*
What's this please? [*point to the menu*]	Τί εἶναι αὐτό παρακαλῶ;
	tee *ee*neh afto parakal*o*
1 kilo of wine	Ἕνα κιλό κρασί
	enna keel*o* krass*ee*
½ kilo of wine	Μισό κιλό κρασί
	m*ee*so keel*o* krass*ee*
¼ kilo of wine	Τέταρτο κρασί
	tetartoh krass*ee*
A glass	Ἕνα ποτήρι
	enna poteeree
A bottle	Ἕνα μπουκάλι
	enna book*a*l-ee
A half bottle	Ἕνα μικρό μπουκάλι
	enna meekr*o* book*a*l-ee
Red/white/rosé	Κόκκινο/ἄσπρο/ροζέ
	kokino/aspro/roz-eh
Some more bread, please	Ἀκόμα ψωμί, παρακαλῶ
	akoma psom-*ee* parakal*o*
Some more wine	ἀκόμα κρασί
	akoma krass*ee*
Some oil	Λίγο λάδι
	l*ee*go l*a*-thee
Some vinegar	Λίγο ξύδι
	l*ee*go ks*ee*-thee
Some salt/pepper	Λίγο ἀλάτι/πιπέρι
	l*ee*go alat-ee/peepeh-ree
With/without garlic	μέ/χωρίς σκόρδο
	meh/hor-*ee*ss skortho
Some water	Λίγο νερό
	l*ee*go nehr*o*
How much does that come to?	Πόσο κάνει;
	posso kan-ee
Is service included	Εἶναι μέ τό σερβίς;
	*ee*neh meh toh serv*ee*ss
Where is the toilet, please?	Ποῦ εἶναι ἡ τουαλέτα, παρακαλῶ;
	poo *ee*neh ee too-al-et-a parakal*o*
Miss! [*This does not sound abrupt in Greek*]	Δεσποινίς!
	thespeen-*ee*ss
Waiter!	Γκαρσόν!
	garson
The bill, please	Τό λογαριασμό, παρακαλῶ
	toh logaree-azmo parakal*o*

Key words for courses, as seen on some menus
[*Only ask this if you want the waiter to remind you of the choice.*]

What have you got in the way of . . .	Τί . . . ἔχετε;
	t*ee* . . . eh-het-eh
STARTERS?	ΟΡΕΚΤΙΚΑ
	or*ekteeka*
SOUP?	ΣΟΥΠΕΣ
	s*oo*pess
EGG?	ΑΥΓΑ
	avg*ah*
FISH?	ΨΑΡΙΑ
	ps*areea*
MEAT?	ΚΡΕΑΣ
	kr*eass*
GAME?	ΚΥΝΗΓΙ
	keen*eegee*
FOWL?	ΠΟΥΛΕΡΙΚΑ
	pool*ereeka*
VEGETABLES?	ΛΑΧΑΝΙΚΑ
	lah*aneeka*
CHEESE?	ΤΥΡΙΑ
	teer*eea*
FRUIT?	ΦΡΟΥΤΑ
	fr*oota*
ICE-CREAM?	ΠΑΓΩΤΑ
	pag*ota*
DESSERT?	ΓΛΥΚΑ
	gleek*a*

UNDERSTANDING THE MENU

You will find the names of the principal ingredients of most dishes on these pages:

Starters	p. 70	Fruit	p. 72
Meat	p. 75	Cheese	p. 70
Fish	p. 77	Ice-cream	p. 66
Vegetables	p. 72	Dessert	p. 64

Used together with the following lists of cooking and menu terms they should help you to decode the menu.

Cooking and mènu terms

Βραστό vrasto	boiled, poached, stewed
γεμιστό ghemeesto	stuffed
ζεστό zesto	hot
καπνιστό kapneesto	smoked
στά κάρβουνα sta karvoona	charcoal-grilled
τῆς κατσαρόλας teess katsar-olass	en casserole
κοκκινιστό kokkin-eesto	cooked with oil and tomatoes
σενιάν (κρέας) sen-yan (kreh-ass)	rare (meat)
μέτρια ψημένο metria pseemen-o	medium
καλοψημένο kalops-eemen-o	well-done
κρύο kree-o	cold
μέ μαϊντανό meh may-dan-o	with parsley
μαρινάτο mareenat-o	marinated
παστό pasto	cured
πουρέ poo-reh	mashed (potatoes)
μέ σάλτσα meh saltsa	with sauce
στή σχάρα stee skar-a	grilled
τηγανισμένο σέ πολύ λάδι teegan-eesmen-o seh pol-ee la-thee	deep fried

τηγανητό	fried
teegan-eeto	
τριμμένο	grated
trimmen-o	
στό φούρνο	baked
sto foorno	
ψητό	roasted, baked
pseeto	
ψητό τῆς κατσαρόλας	pot-roasted
pseeto teess katsar-olass	
ψηλοκομμένο	finely chopped
psee-lokommen-o	
ὠμό	raw
om-o	

Further words to help you understand the menu

ἀγγούρι	cucumber
angooree	
αὐγολέμονο	rice, egg and lemon soup
avgol-em-ono	
γαριδοσαλάτα	shrimps in oil and lemon sauce
gareeth-osala-ta	
γιουβαρλάκια	minced meat and rice balls
yoo-varlak-ya	
γιουβέτσι	meat with noodles baked in the oven
yoo-vet-see	
κεφτέδες	meatballs made with bread and herbs
kefteth-ess	
κοκορέτσι	lamb innards roasted on a spit
kokoret-see	
κρεμμύδι	onion
kremmeethee	
μελιτζάνες γεμιστές	stuffed aubergines
mel-eetzan-ess ghe-meess-tess	
μουσακά	layers of baked aubergines and minced meat
moossaka	
μπιζέλια	peas
beezel-ya	
μπιφτέκια	grilled meatballs
beeftekya	
ντολμάδες	vine or cabbage leaves stuffed with rice and/or meat
dolmath-ess	

ντομάτες γεμιστές
domat-ess ghemeess-tess
: stuffed tomatoes with rice and/or minced meat

παστίτσιο
pasteetsio
: minced meat and macaroni baked and completed by a sauce

παστουρμάς
pastoorm-ass
: heavily spiced, dried or smoked meat

πατσάς
patsass
: tripe soup

πιπεριές γεμιστές
peepeh-ree-ess ghemeess-tess
: stuffed peppers

ρεβύθια
reh-veethia
: chick-peas

σκορδαλιά
skor-thal-ya
: garlic sauce

σκόρδο
skortho
: garlic

σουβλάκι
soovlak-ee
: cubes of meat grilled on a spit

σουτζουκάκια
soot-zookak-ya
: spicy meatballs in sauce

ταραμοσαλάτα
taramo-sala-ta
: salad of fish roe blended with bread, oil and lemon

τζατζίκι
tsat-zeekee
: salad of yoghurt, cucumber, garlic, olive oil and mint

φακιές
fak-yess
: lentils

φασολάδα
fassol-atha
: kidney bean soup with tomatoes

χόρτα σαλάτα
horta sala-ta
: made from greens resembling spinach

χυλόπιττες
heelop-eet-ess
: noodles

χωριάτικη σαλάτα
horeeat-eekee sala-ta
: mixed salad, (tomatoes, cucumber, green peppers, cheese, onion)

ψαρόσουπα
psaross-oopa
: fish soup

Health

ESSENTIAL INFORMATION

- At present there are no reciprocal health agreements between the UK and Greece. Moreover, the public health sector offers an extremely limited service. It is *essential* to have proper medical insurance. A policy can be bought through a travel agent, a broker or a motoring organization.
- Take your own 'first line' first aid kit with you.
- See p. 44 for minor disorders and treatment at a chemist's.
- See p. 22 for asking the way to a doctor, dentist, or chemist.
- Once in Greece decide on a definite plan of action in case of serious illness: communicate your problem to a near neighbour, the receptionist or someone you see regularly. You are then dependent on that person helping you obtain treatment.
- To find a doctor in an emergency look for: ΝΟΣΟΚΟΜΕΙΟΝ (hospital) or contact the police.
- Because of the limited ambulance service in Greece, taxis are frequently used to take people to hospital.

What's the matter?

I have a pain in my . . .	Μοῦ πονάει . . .
	moo pona-ee. . .
abdomen	τό στομάχι
	toh stomahee
ankle	ὁ ἀστράγαλος
	o astragal-oss
arm	τό χέρι
	toh hehree
back	ἡ πλάτη
	ee plat-ee
bladder	ἡ κύστις
	ee keesteess
bowels	τό ἔντερο
	toh endero
breast/chest	τό στῆθος
	toh steethoss
ear	τό αὐτί
	toh aftee

eye	τό μάτι
	toh mat-ee
foot	τό πόδι
	toh poth-ee
head	τό κεφάλι
	toh kef-al-ee
heel	ἡ φτέρνα
	ee ftehr-na
jaw	τό σαγώνι
	toh sag-on-ee
kidney	τό νεφρό
	toh nefro
leg	τό πόδι
	toh po-thee
lung	ὁ πνεύμων
	o pnevmon
neck	ὁ λαιμός
	o lem-oss
penis	τό πέος
	toh peh-oss
shoulder	ἡ ὠμοπλάτη
	ee omo-plat-ee
stomach	τό στομάχι
	toh stoma-hee
testicle	ὁ ὄρχις
	o orheess
throat	ὁ λαιμός
	o lem-oss
vagina	ὁ κόλπος
	o kolposs
wrist	ὁ καρπός τοῦ χεριοῦ
	o karposs too hehr-ee-oo
I have a pain here [*point*]	Ἔχω ἕνα πόνο ἐδῶ
	eh-ho enna pon-o eth-o
I have toothache	Ἔχω πονόδοντο
	eh-ho pon-othondo
I have broken . . .	Ἔσπασα . . .
	espassa . . .
my dentures	τή μασέλα μου
	tee massella moo
my glasses	τά γυαλιά μου
	ta yal-ya moo

I have lost . . .	Ἔχασα . . . eh-hassa . . .
my contact lenses	τούς φακούς ἐπαφῆς μου tooss fak-ooss ep-afeess moo
a filling	ἔνα σφράγισμα enna sfrag-eesma
My child is ill	Τό παιδί μου εἶναι ἄρρωστο toh peth-ee moo eeneh arrosto
He/she has a pain in his/her. . .	Τοῦ/Τῆς πονάει . . . too/teess pona-ee . . .
ankle [see list above]	ὁ ἀστράγαλος o astragal-oss
How bad is it?	
I'm ill	Εἶμαι ἄρρωστος/ἄρρωστη* eemeh arrostoss/arrostee*
It's urgent	Εἶναι ἐπεῖγον eeneh ep-eegon
It's serious	Εἶναι σοβαρό eeneh sovaro
It's not serious	Δέν εἶναι σοβαρό then eeneh sovaro
It hurts	Πονάει pona-ee
It hurts a lot	Πονάει πολύ pona-ee pol-ee
It doesn't hurt much	Δέν πονάει πολύ then pona-ee pol-ee
The pain occurs . . .	Ὁ πόνος ἔρχεται . . . o pon-oss ehr-het-eh . . .
every quarter of an hour	κάθε τέταρτο kath-eh tet-arto
every half hour	κάθε μισύ ὥρα kath-eh meessee ora
every hour	κάθε ὥρα kath-eh ora
every day	κάθε μέρα kath-eh mehra
most of the time	τίς περισσότερες φορές teess perissot-ehress for-ess
I've had it for . . .	Τόν ἔχω ἐδῶ καί . . . ton eh-ho eth-o keh . . .

*For men use the first alternative, for women the second

one hour/one day	μία ὥρα/μία μέρα
	mee-a ora/mee-a mehra
two hours/two days	δύο ὧρες/δύο μέρες
	thee-o or-ess/thee-o mehr-ess
It's a ...	Εἶναι ἕνας ...
	eeneh ennass ...
sharp pain	ξαφνικός πόνος
	ksaf-neek-oss pon-oss
dull pain	μέτριος πόνος
	met-ree-os pon-oss
nagging pain	ἐνοχλητικός πόνος
	enno-hleet-eekoss pon-oss
I feel ...	Αἰσθάνομαι ...
	es-than-om-eh ...
dizzy	μία ζάλη
	mee-a zal-ee
sick	μία τάση γιά ἐμετό
	mee-a tassee ya em-et-o
weak	μία ἀδυναμία
	mee-a a-theen-amee-ya
feverish	νά ἔχω πυρετό
	na eh-ho peeret-o

Already under treatment for something else?

I take ... regularly [show]	Παίρνω συνήθως ...
	pehr-no seeneeth-oss ...
this medicine	αὐτό τό φάρμακο
	afto toh farmako
these pills	αὐτά τά χάπια
	afta ta hap-ya
I have ...	Ἔχω ...
	eh-ho ...
haemorrhoids	αἱμορροΐδες
	em-orro-eethess
rheumatism	ρευματισμούς
	revma-teezmooss
I'm ...	Εἶμαι ...
	eemeh ...
diabetic	διαβητικός/διαβητική*
	thee-av-eeteek-oss/thee-av-eeteek-ee*

*For men use the first alternative, for women the second

I'm ... Εἶμαι ...
eemeh ...

  asthmatic ἀσθματικός/ἀσθματική*
as-thmat-eek-oss/as-thmat-eek-ee*

  pregnant ἔγκυος
engee-oss

I have a heart condition Εἶμαι καρδιακός/καρδιακή*.
eemeh karthee-akoss/karthee-akee*

I am allergic to (pencillin) Εἶμαι ἀλλεργικός/ἀλλεργική* στή
(πενικιλλίνη)
eemeh allehr-geek-oss/
allehr-geek-ee stee
(pen-eekeel-eenee)

Other essential expressions

Please can you help? Μπορεῖτε νά με βοηθήσετε σᾶς
παρακαλῶ;
boreeteh na meh vo-eeth-eesset-eh
sas parakalo

A doctor, please Ἕνα γιατρό, παρακαλῶ
enna yatro parakalo

A dentist Ἕνα ὀδοντογιατρό
enna othondo-yatro

I don't speak Greek Δέν μιλῶ Ἑλληνικά
then meelo elleen-eeka

What time does ... arrive? Τί ὥρα ἔρχεται ...
tee ora erheteh ...

  the doctor ὁ γιατρός;
o yatross

  the dentist ὁ ὀδοντογιατρός;
o othondo-yatross

From the doctor: key sentences to understand

Take this ... Νά παίρνετε αὐτό ...
na pehr-net-eh afto ...

  every day/hour κάθε μέρα/ὥρα
kath-eh mehra/ora

  twice/four times a day δύο/τέσσερες φορές τή μέρα
thee-o/tesser-ess for-ess tee mer-a

Stay in bed Μείνετε στό κρεββάτι
meenet-eh sto krevvat-ee

*For men use the first alternative, for women the second

Don't travel	Μή ταξιδεύετε
	mee taksee-theh-vet-eh
for . . . days/weeks	γιά . . . μέρες/βδομάδες
	ya . . . mehr-ess/vthom-ath-ess
You must go to hospital	Πρέπει νά πᾶτε στό νοσοκομείο
	prep-ee na pat-eh sto nossokomee-o

Problems: complaints, loss, theft

ESSENTIAL INFORMATION

- Problems with:
  camping facilities, see p. 38.
  household appliances, see p. 41.
  health, see p. 90
  the car, see p. 104.
- If the worst comes to the worst, find the police station, to ask the way, see p. 22.
- Look for:
  ΑΣΤΥΝΟΜΙΑ (police in towns) or this sign

or ΧΩΡΟΦΥΛΑΚΗ (gendarmerie, i.e. rural police)
- If you lose your passport go to the nearest British Consulate.
- In an emergency, dial 100 for the police.

COMPLAINTS

I bought this . . .	Ἀγόρασα αὐτό . . .
	agorassa afto . . .
today	σήμερα
	seemera
yesterday	χθές
	hthess
on Monday [see p. 129]	τή Δευτέρα
	tee theftehra
It's no good	Δέν εἶναι καλό
	then eeneh kalo
Look	Κυττάξτε
	keetaks-teh
Here [point]	Ἐδῶ
	eth-o
Can you . . .	Μπορεῖτε νά τό . . .
	boreeteh na toh . . .
change it?	ἀλλάξετε;
	allak-set-eh
mend it?	Ἐπισκευάσετε;
	ep-eeskev-asset-eh
Here's the receipt	Ὁρίστε ἡ ἀπόδειξη
	oreesteh ee apotheek-see
Can I have a refund?	Μπορεῖτε νά μοῦ ἐπιστρέψετε τά χρήματα;
	boreeteh na moo ep-eestrepset-eh ta hreemata
Can I see the manager?	Μπορῶ νά δῶ τόν διευθυντή;
	boro na tho ton thee-ef-theen-tee

LOSS
[See also 'Theft' below; the lists are interchangeable]

I have lost . . .	Ἔχασα . . .
	eh-hassa . . .
my bag	τήν τσάντα μου
	teen tsanda moo
my bracelet	τό βραχιόλι μου
	toh vra-hee-olee moo
my camera	τήν φωτογραφική μηχανή μου
	teen fotograffeekee meehanee moo
my car logbook	τήν ἄδεια κυκλοφορίας
	teen ath-eya keek-loforee-ass

my driving licence	τήν ἄδεια ὁδηγήσεως
	teen athee-a othee-geess-eh-oss
my insurance certificate	τήν ἀσφάλεια τοῦ αὐτοκινήτου μου
	teen asfal-ya too aftokeen-eetoo moo
my jewellery	τά κοσμήματα μου
	ta kosmeem-ata moo
everything	τά πάντα
	ta panda

THEFT
[See also 'Loss' above; the lists are interchangeable]

Someone has stolen ...	Κάποιος μοῦ ἔκλεψε ...
	kap-ee-oss moo eklepseh ...
my car	τό αὐτοκίνητο μου
	toh aftokeen-eeto moo
my car radio	Τό ράδιό τοῦ αὐτοκινήτου μου
	toh rath-yo too aftokokeen-eetoo moo
my car keys	τά κλειδιά τοῦ αὐτοκινήτου μου
	ta kleeth-ya too aftokeen-eetoo moo
my keys	τά κλειδιά μου
	ta kleeth-ya moo
my money	τά χρήματα μου
	ta hreem-ata moo
my necklace	τό κολλιέ μου
	toh kollee-eh moo
my passport	τό διαβατήριο μου
	toh thee-avateeree-o moo
my radio	τό ράδιο μου
	toh rath-yo moo
my tickets	τά εἰσιτήρια μου
	ta eess-eeteeree-a moo
my travellers' cheques	τά τράβελερς τσέκς μου
	ta travellers' cheques moo
my wallet	τό πορτοφόλι μου
	toh portofol-ee moo
my watch	τό ρολόϊ μου
	toh rolo-ee moo
my luggage	τά πράγματα μου
	ta pragmata moo

LIKELY REACTIONS: key words to understand

Wait	Περιμένετε
	perimen-et-eh
When?	Πότε;
	pot-eh
Where?	Πού;
	poo
Name?	Όνομα;
	onoma
Address?	Διεύθυνση;
	thee-ef-theen-see
I can't help you	Δέν μπορῶ νά σᾶς βοηθήσω
	then boro na sas vo-ee-theessa
Nothing to do with me	Δέν μπορῶ νά κάνω τίποτα
	then boro na kano teepota

The post office

ESSENTIAL INFORMATION

- To find a post office, see p. 22.
- Key words to look for:
  ΤΑΧΥΔΡΟΜΕΙΟΝ (post office)
  ΕΛ.ΤΑ, (abbreviation for Greek
  post office: look out for this symbol)
  ΟΤΕ (telecommunications)
- For stamps, look for the word
  ΓΡΑΜΜΑΤΟΣΗΜΑ.
- Stamps are also sold in kiosks.
- Letter boxes are yellow.
- For post restante you should show
  your passport at the counter marked
  ΠΟΣΤ ΡΕΣΤΑΝΤ in the main post office.
- Telegrams are not sent from post offices, but from the offices of
  the OTE, the telecommunications company of Greece.

WHAT TO SAY

To England, please	Γιά τήν 'Αγγλία, παρακαλῶ
	ya teen anglee-a parakalo

[*Hand letters, cards or parcels over the counter*]

To Australia	Γιά τήν Αὐστραλία
	ya teen af-straleea
To the United States	Γιά τήν 'Αμερική
	ya teen amerik-ee

[*For other countries, see p. 134*]

How much is . . .	Πόσο κάνει . . .
	posso kan-ee . . .
this parcel (to Canada)?	αὐτό τό δέμα (γιά τόν Καναδᾶ);
	afto toh them-a (ya ton kana-tha)
a letter (to Australia)?	ἕνα γράμμα (γιά τήν Αὐστραλία);
	enna gramma (ya teen af-stralee-a)
a postcard (to England)?	μία κάρτα (γιά τήν 'Αγγλία);
	mee-a karta (ya teen anglee-a)
Airmail	'Αεροπορικῶς
	ehroporeek-oss
Surface mail	'Απλό
	aplo
One stamp, please	Ἕνα γραμματόσημο, παρακαλῶ
	enna grammat-oss-eemo parakalo
Two stamps	Δύο γραμματόσημα
	thee-o grammat-oss-eema
One (10) drachma stamp	Ἕνα γραμματόσημο (τῶν δέκα) δραχμῶν
	enna grammat-oss-eemo (ton theh-ka) thra-hmon

Telephoning

ESSENTIAL INFORMATION

- Unless you read and speak Greek well, it's best not to make phone calls by yourself. Go to OTE (Telecommunications Organization of Greece, look out for this symbol) – and not to the post office – and write the town and number you want on a piece of paper.
- Add ΠΡΟΣΩΠΙΚΟ ΤΗΛΕΦΩΝΗΜΑ if you want a person-to-person call, or ΝΑ ΧΡΕΩΘΕΙ ΤΟ ΤΗΛΕΦΩΝΗΜΑ ΣΤΟΝ ΠΑΡ-ΑΛΗΠΤΗ if you want to reverse the charges.
- The number of public phones is rather limited in Greece. How-ever, almost all kiosks and a number of cafés have phones for the public. Phones in cafés have meters and you pay after phoning according to the number of units used. The few public phone boxes are blue for local calls and orange for long distance and use normal currency not tokens.
- To ask the way to a telephone, see p. 22.
- Look for these signs:
  ΤΗΛΕΦΩΝΟ ΔΙΑ ΤΟ ΚΟΙΝΟ (public telephone)
  ΕΔΩ ΤΗΛΕΦΩΝΕΙΤΕ (telephone here)
- OTE phones must be used for all international calls.
- To phone the UK from Greece, dial 0044 and then the number you want.
- To phone the USA, the code is 001.
- You can ask at your local post office before leaving for a brochure on phoning England from abroad.

WHAT TO SAY

Where can I make a telphone call?	Πού μπορῶ νά κάνω ἕνα τηλέφωνο;
	poo boro na kan-o enna teelefono
Local/abroad	Τοπικό/γιά τό ἐξωτερικό
	top-eeko/ya toh eksot-ehreeko

I'd like this number . . .	Θέλω αὐτό τόν ἀριθμό . . .
[show number]	thello af*to* ton a-reethm*o* . . .
in England	στήν Ἀγγλία
	steen angle*ea*
in Canada	στόν Καναδᾶ
	ston kana-th*a*
in the USA	στήν Ἀμερική
	steen amerik-*ee*
[For other countries, see p. 134]	
Can you dial it for me, please?	Μπορεῖτε νά μοῦ πάρετε τόν ἀριθμό, σᾶς παρακαλῶ;
	bor*ee*teh na moo par-et-eh ton a-reethm*o* sas parakal*o*
How much is it?	Πόσο κάνει;
	posso kan-ee
Hello	Ναί
	neh
May I speak to . . .?	Μοῦ δίνετε . . .;
	moo th*ee*net-eh . . .
Extension . . .	Ἐσωτερικό . . .
	es-otehreek*o* . . .
I'm sorry, I don't speak Greek	Λυπᾶμαι, δέν μιλάω Ἑλληνικά
	leep*am*-eh then meela-o elleen-eek*a*
Do you speak English?	Μιλᾶτε Ἀγγλικά;
	meelat-eh angleek*a*
Goodbye	Χαίρετε
	h*e*h-ret-eh
I'd like to send a telegram	Θέλω νά στείλω ἔνα τηλεγράφημα
	thello na st*ee*lo *e*nna teelegraf-eema

LIKELY REACTIONS

That's (45) drachmas	(Σαράντα πέντε) δραχμές
	(saranda pendeh) thra-hmess
Cabin number (3)	Θάλαμος νουμερο (τρία)
[For numbers, see p. 125]	thalamoss n*oo*mero (treea)
Don't hang up	Μήν κλείσετε
	meen kl*ee*sset-eh

I'm trying to connect you	Προσπαθῶ νά σᾶς συνδέσω
	prospatho na sas seen-theh-so
You're through	Μιλᾶτε
	meelat-eh
There's a delay	Ὑπάρχει καθυστέρηση
	eepar-hee kathee-stehr-eessee
I'll try again	Θά προσπαθήσω ξανά
	tha prospatheesso ksana

Changing cheques and money

ESSENTIAL INFORMATION

- Finding your way to a bank of change bureau, see p. 22.
- Look for these signs:
  ΤΡΑΠΕΖΑ (bank)
  BUREAU DE CHANGE (change bureau)
- To cash your normal cheques, exactly as at home, use your banker's card where you see the Eurocheque sign. Write in English, in pounds.
- Exchange rate information shows the pound as: £. It is also quite often simply shown by the British flag.
- Have your passport handy.
- Banks are open between 8.00 a.m. and 2.00 p.m. except on Saturdays, Sundays and public holidays. However, during the high season some banks will remain open during the afternoons.

WHAT TO SAY

I'd like to cash . . .	Θέλω νά ἐξαργυρώσω . . .
	thello na ek-sarg-eerosso . . .
this travellers' cheque	αὐτό τό τράβελερς τσέκ
	afto toh travellers' cheque
these travellers' cheques	αὐτά τά τράβελερς τσέκ
	afta ta travellers' cheques
this cheque	αὐτό τό τσέκ
	afto toh cheque

I'd like to change this into drachmas	Θά ἤθελα νά αλλάξω αὐτό σέ δραχμές
	tha eethella na allakso afto seh thra-hmess
Here's . . .	Ὁρίστε . . .
	oreesteh . . .
my banker's card	ἡ τραπεζική μου κάρτα
	ee trap-ez-eekee moo karta
my passport	τό διαβατήριο μου
	toh thee-avateeree-o moo

For excursions into neighbouring countries

I'd like to change this . . . [show banknotes]	Θέλω νά ἀλλάξω αὐτό . . .
	thello na allakso afto . . .
into Italian lira	σέ Ἰταλικές λιρέττες
	seh eetal-eekess leeret-ess
into Turkish pounds	σέ τούρκικες λίρες
	seh toor-keekess leeress
into Yugoslav dinar	σέ γιουγκοσλαυικά δηνάρια
	seh yoogoslavika deenareeya
What is the rate of exchange?	Ποία εἶναι ἡ τιμή συναλλάγματος;
	peea eeneh ee teemee seen-allagmat-oss

LIKELY REACTIONS

Passport, please	Τό διαβατήριο σας, παρακαλῶ
	toh thee-avateeree-o sas parakalo
Sign here	Ὑπογράψετε ἐδῶ
	eepograp-set-eh eth-o
Your banker's card, please	Τήν τραπεζική σας κάρτα, παρακαλῶ
	teen trap-ez-eekee sas karta parakalo
Go to the cash desk	Πηγαίνετε στό ταμεῖο
	peeg-en-et-eh sto tam-ee-o

Car travel

ESSENTIAL INFORMATION

- Finding a filling station or garage, see p. 22.
- Is it a self-service filling station? Look out for:
  ΣΕΛΦ-ΣΕΡΒΙΣ
- Grades of petrol: ΣΟΥΠΕΡ (premium)
  BENZINH (petrol)   ΔΙΧΡΟΝΟ (two stroke)
  ΑΠΛΗ (standard)   ΝΤΗΖΕΛ (diesel)
- One gallon is about 4½ litres (accurate enough up to 6 gallons).
- Most filling stations in Greece (ΓΚΑΡΑΖ) do not do major repairs. The place to go to for repairs is ΣΥΝΕΡΓΕΙΟΝ
- Holders of British driving licences do not need an international driving licence.
- The Greek Automobile and Touring Club (ELPA) offers assistance to foreign motorists free of charge.
- Dial 104 for assistance in Athens and Thessaloniki (up to a radius of 60 km) and Larissa, Patras, Herakleion, Volos, Lamia, Kalamata and Yannina (up to a radius of 25 km).
- Unfamiliar road signs and warnings, see p. 119.

WHAT TO SAY
[For numbers, see p. 125]

(Nine) litres of . . .	(Ἐννέα) λίτρα . . .
	(enneh-a) leetra . . .
(150) drachmas of . . .	(ἑκατό πενῆντα) δραχμές . . .
	(ek-at-o pen-eenda) thra-hmess ; . .
standard	ἁπλή
	aplee
premium	σοῦπερ
	soopehr
diesel	ντῆζελ
	diesel
Fill it up, please	Νά τό γεμίσετε, παρακαλῶ
	na toh gemeesset-eh, parakalo
Will you check . . .	Μπορεῖτε νά κοιτάξετε . . .
	boreeteh na keetak-set-eh . . .
the oil	τό λάδι
	toh la-thee

the battery	τήν μπαταρία
	teen bataree-a
the radiator	τό ψυγείο
	toh pseeg-ee-o
the tyres	τά λάστιχα
	ta lastee-ha
I've run out of petrol	Ἔμεινα ἀπό πετρέλαιο
	em-eena apo petrel-eh-o
Can I borrow a can, please?	Μοῦ δανείζετε ἔνα δοχείο βενζίνης, παρακαλῶ;
	moo than-eezet-eh enna tho-hee-o venzeen-eess parakalo
My car has broken down	Χάλασε τό αὐτοκίνητο μου
	halasseh toh aftokeen-eeto moo
My car won't start	Τό αὐτοκίνητο μου δέν ξεκινάει
	toh aftokeen-eeto moo then ksek-eena-ee
I've had an accident	Εἴχα ἔνα ἀτύχημα
	ee-ha enna a-tee-heema
I've lost my car keys	Ἔχασα τά κλειδιά τοῦ αὐτοκινήτου μου
	eh-hassa ta kleeth-ya too aftokeen-eetoo moo
My car is . . .	Τό αὐτοκίνητο μου εἴναι . . .
	toh aftokeen-eeto moo eeneh . . .
two kilometres away	δύο χιλιόμετρα ἀπό ἐδῶ
	thee-o heelee-ometra apo eth-o
three kilometres away	τρία χιλιόμετρα ἀπό ἐδῶ
	tree-a heelee-ometra apo eth-o
Can you help me, please?	Μπορείτε νά μέ βοηθήσετε, σᾶς παρακαλῶ;
	boreeteh na meh vo-eeth-eeset-eh sas parakalo
Do you do repairs?	Κάνετε ἐπισκευές;
	kan-et-eh ep-eeskev-ess
I have a puncture	Τρύπησε τό λάστιχο
	treepees-eh toh lastee-ho
I have a broken windscreen	Ἔσπασε τό μπροστινό τζάμι
	espas-eh toh brosteeno tzam-ee
I think the problem is here . . . [point]	Νομίζω ὅτι τό πρόβλημα εἴναι ἐδῶ . . .
	nomeezo otee toh prov-leema eeneh eth-o

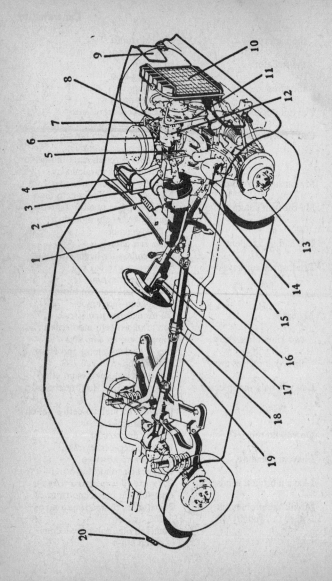

1 windscreen wipers	ὑαλοκαθαριστῆρες	ee-alok-athar-eesteer-ess
2 fuses	ἀσφάλεια	asfalee-a
3 heater	καλοριφέρ	kaloreef-ehr
4 battery	μπαταρία	bataree-a
5 engine	μοτέρ	motehr
6 fuel pump	ἀντλία βενζίνης	antlee-a venzeen-eess
7 starter motor	στάρτερ	startehr
8 carburettor	καρμπυρατέρ	karbeera-tehr
9 lights	τά φῶτα	ta fota
10 radiator	ψυγείο	pseeg-ee-o
11 fan belt	λουρί	loo-ree
12 generator	γεννήτρια	ghe-neetri-a
13 brakes	φρένα	frenna
14 clutch	συμπλέκτης	seeblek-teess
15 gear box	κιβώτιο ταχυτήτων	keevot-yo ta-heeteeton
16 steering	τιμόνι	teemon-ee
17 ignition	μίζα	meeza
18 transmission	μετάδοση	met-athoss-ee
19 exhaust	ἐξάτμιση	eksat-meessee
20 indicators	φλάς	flass

I don't know what's wrong	Δέν ξέρω τί ἔχει
	then ksehr-o tee eh-hee
Can you . . .	Μπορειτε νά . . .
	boreeteh na . . .
repair the fault?	τό ἐπισκευάσετε;
	toh ep-eeskev-asset-eh
come and look?	ἔρθετε νά τό δεῖτε;
	ehr-thet-eh na toh theeteh
estimate the cost?	μοῦ πῆτε πόσο θά κάνει;
	moo peeteh posso tha kanee
write it down?	τό γράψετε;
	toh grapset-eh
Do you accept these coupons?	Δέχεστε αὐτά τά κουπόνια;
	theh-hess-teh afta ta koopon-ya
How long will the repair take?	Πόσο θά σᾶς πάρει νά τό ἐπισκευάσετε;
	posso tha sas par-ee na toh ep-eess-kehv-asset-eh
When will the car be ready?	Πότε θά εἶναι ἕτοιμο τό αὐτοκίνητο;
	pot-eh tha eeneh et-eemo toh aftokeen-eeto
Can I see the bill?	Μπορῶ νά δῶ τό λογαριασμό;
	boro na tho toh logaree-azmo
This is my insurance document	Ὁρίστε ἡ ἀσφάλεια μου
	oreesteh ee asfal-ya moo

HIRING A CAR

Can I hire a car?	Μπορῶ νά νοικιάσω ἕνα αὐτοκίνητο;
	boro na neek-yasso enna aftokeen-eeto
I need a car . . .	Θέλω ἕνα αὐτοκίνητο . . .
	thello enna aftokeen-eeto. . .
for two people	γιά δύο ἄτομα
	ya thee-o atoma
for five people	γιά πέντε ἄτομα
	ya pendeh atoma
for one day	γιά μία μέρα
	ya mee-a mehra
for five days	γιά πέντε μέρες
	ya pendeh mehress

for a week	γιά μία βδομάδα
	ya mee-a vthoma-tha
Can you write down . . .	Μοῦ γράφετε . . .
	moo graf-et-eh . . .
the deposit to pay?	τήν προκαταβολή;
	teen prokatavol-ee
the charge per kilometre?	πόσο κάνει τό χιλιόμετρο;
	posso kan-ee toh heelee-ometro
the daily charge?	πόσο κάνει τήν ἡμέρα;
	posso kan-ee teen eem-ehra
the cost of insurance?	πόσο κάνει ἡ ἀσφάλεια;
	posso kan-ee ee asfal-ya
Can I leave it (in Athens)?	Μπορῶ νά τό ἀφήσω (στήν Ἀθήνα);
	boro na toh a-feeso (steen athee-na)
What documents do I need?	Τί ἔγγραφα χρειάζομαι;
	tee eng-rafa hree-az-om-eh

LIKELY REACTIONS

I don't do repairs	Δέν κάνω ἐπισκευές
	then kan-o ep-eeskev-ess
Where's your car?	Ποῦ εἶναι τό αὐτοκίνητο σας;
	poo eeneh toh aftokeen-eeto sas
What make is it?	Τί μάρκα εἶναι;
	tee marka eeneh
Come back tomorrow/on Monday	Ἐλᾶτε αὔριο/τή Δευτέρα
	ellat-eh avrio/tee thef-tehra

[*For days of the week, see p. 129*]

We don't hire cars	Δέν νοικιάζουμε αὐτοκίνητα
	then neek-yaz-oom-eh aftokeen-eeta
Your driving licence, please	Τήν ἄδεια ὁδηγήσεως, παρακαλῶ
	teen ath-ya o-thee-geesseh-oss parakalo
The mileage is unlimited	Δέν ὑπάρχει μίνιμουμ χιλιομετρικό ὅριο
	then eepar-hee minimum heelee-ometreek-o oree-o

Public transport

ESSENTIAL INFORMATION

- Finding the way to the bus station, a bus stop, a trolley stop, the railway station and a taxi rank, see p. 22.
- Remember that queuing for buses is not strictly followed.
- The railway network in Greece is not very extensive. The national railways connect Athens with the most important regions of the country. Buses are more frequent (much faster than trains).
- The underground in Athens is called Ό ΗΛΕΚΤΡΙΚΟΣ, and joins Piraeus with Athens and Kifissia.
- There are frequent ferry-boats to most islands from Piraeus.
- In Athens there are electric trolleys in addition to the bus services. For urban buses and trolleys there is a flat rate which you pay to the conductor. Some of these have no conductors, so no change is available and you drop the fare into a box. They have a large sign on the front: ΧΩΡΙΣ ΕΙΣΠΡΑΚΤΟΡΑ (without conductor) and you get in and pay at the front and get out at the back.
- Key words on signs: (see also p. 119)
  ΓΡΑΦΕΙΟΝ ΕΙΣΙΤΗΡΙΩΝ (ticket office)
  ΕΙΣΟΔΟΣ (entrance)
  ΑΠΑΓΟΡΕΥΕΤΑΙ Η ΕΙΣΟΔΟΣ (no entrance)
  ΑΝΟΔΟΣ (entrance, for buses)
  ΚΑΘΟΔΟΣ (exit, for buses)
  ΠΡΟΣ ΤΑΣ ΑΠΟΒΑΘΡΑΣ (to the platforms)
  ΓΡΑΦΕΙΟΝ ΠΛΗΡΟΦΟΡΙΩΝ (information office)
  ΟΣΕ (initials for Greek railways)
  ΚΤΕΛ (initials for Greek coach services)
  ΕΞΟΔΟΣ (exit)
  ΘΥΡΙΔΕΣ ΑΠΟΣΚΕΥΩΝ (left luggage)
  ΣΤΑΣΙΣ stop: in Athens the stops are yellow for trolleys and blue for buses. The sign shows a bus stop.
  ΔΡΟΜΟΛΟΓΙΟΝ
  (timetable)

WHAT TO SAY

Where does the ferry-boat for (Piraeus) leave from?	Ἀπό ποῦ φεύγει τό φέρυ μπότ γιά τόν (Πειραιᾶ);
	apo poo fev-ghee toh ferry-boat ya ton (peereya)
At what time does the ferry-boat leave for (Piraeus)?	Τί ὥρα φεύγει τό φέρυ μπότ γιά τόν (Πειραιᾶ);
	tee ora fev-ghee toh ferry-boat ya ton (peereya)
At what time does the ferry-boat arrive in (Piraeus)?	Τί ὥρα φτάνει τό φέρυ μπότ στόν (Πειραιᾶ);
	tee ora ftan-ee toh ferry-boat ston (peereya)
Is this the ferry-boat for (Piraeus)?	Εἶναι αὐτό τό φερυ μπότ γιά τόν (Πειραιᾶ);
	eeneh afto toh ferry-boat ya ton (peereya)
Where does the bus for (Delphi) leave from?	Ἀπό ποῦ φεύγει τό λεωφορεῖο γιά τούς (Δελφούς);
	apo poo fev-ghee toh leh-oforee-o ya tooss (thelfooss)
At what time does the bus leave for (Delphi)?	Τί ὥρα φεύγει τό λεωφορεῖο γιά τούς (Δελφούς);
	tee ora fev-ghee toh leh-oforee-o ya tooss (thelfooss)
At what time does the bus arrive at (Delphi)?	Τί ὥρα φτάνει τό λεωφορεῖο στούς (Δελφούς);
	tee ora ftan-ee toh leh-oforee-o stooss (thelfooss)
Is this the bus for (Delphi)?	Αὐτό εἶναι τό λεωφορεῖο γιά τούς (Δελφούς);
	afto eeneh toh leh-oforee-o ya tooss (thelfooss)
Do I have to change?	Πρέπει νά ἀλλάξω;
	prep-ee na allak-so
Where does . . . leave from?	Ἀπό ποῦ φεύγει . . .
	apo poo fev-ghee
the bus	τό λεωφορεῖο;
	toh leh-oforee-o
the train	τό τραῖνο;
	toh tren-o
the underground	ὁ ἠλεκτρικός;
	o eelek-treekoss

Where does . . . leave from?	Ἀπό ποῦ φεύγει . . . ap*o poo* fev-ghee
the ferry-boat	τό φέρυ μπότ toh ferry-boat
for the airport	γιά τό ἀεροδρόμιο; ya toh ehr-othrom-yo
for the beach	γιά τήν παραλία; ya teen paral*ee*-a
for the market place	γιά τήν ἀγορά; ya ton agor*ah*
for the railway station	γιά τό σιδηροδρομικό σταθμό; ya toh see-theer-othrom-eeko stathmo
for the town centre	γιά τό κέντρο τῆς πόλης; ya toh kendro teess pol-eess
for St Dimitrios' church	γιά τόν Ἅγιο Δημήτριο; ya ton *a*g-yo thee-meetrio
for the swimming pool	γιά τήν πισίνα; ya teen pee-seena
Is this . . .	Αὐτό εἶναι . . . afto *ee*neh . . .

the bus for the market
     place?
	τό λεωφορειο γιά τήν ἀγορά;
	     toh leh-ofor*ee*-o ya teen agor*ah*

the trolley for the railway
     station?
	τό τρολλεϋ γιά τό σιδηροδρομικό
	     σταθμό;
	     toh trolley ya toh see-theer-
	          othromeeko stathmo

Where can I get a taxi?	Ποῦ μπορῶ νά βρῶ ἕνα ταξί; poo boro na vro enna taksee
Can you put me off at the right stop, please?	Μπορεῖτε νά μέ κατεβάσετε στή σωστή στάση, παρακαλῶ; boreeteh na meh kat-ev-asset-eh stee sostee stassee parakalo
Can I book a seat?	Μπορῶ νά κλείσω μιά θέση; boro na kleesso mee-a thessee
A single	Ἕνα ἁπλό εἰσιτήριο enna aplo eess-eeteerio
A return	Ἕνα εἰσιτήριο μετ'ἐπιστροφῆς enna eess-eeteerio met-ep-eestr-of-eess
First class	Πρώτη θέση prot-ee thess-ee

Second class	Δεύτερη θέση
	thef-tehree thessee
One adult	Ἕνας ἐνήλικας
	ennas en-eeleek-ass
Two adults	Δύο ἐνήλικες
	thee-o en-eeleek-ess
and one child	καί ἕνα παιδί
	keh enna peth-ee
and two children	καί δύο παιδιά
	keh thee-o peth-ya
How much is it?	Πόσο κάνει;
	posso kan-ee

LIKELY REACTIONS

Over there	Ἐκεῖ
	ek-ee
Here	Ἐδῶ
	eth-o
Platform (1)	Πλατφόρμα νούμερο (ἕνα)
	platforma noomero (enna)
At (four o'clock)	Στίς (τέσσερεις)
[For times, see p. 127]	steess (tesser-eess)
Change at (Lamia)	Νά ἀλλάξετε στή (Λαμία)
	na allak-set-eh stee (lam-ee-a)
Change at (the town hall)	Νά ἀλλάξετε (στό Δημαρχείο)
	na allak-set-eh (sto theemar-hee-o)
This is your stop	Αὐτή εἶναι ἡ στάση σας
	aftee eeneh ee stassee sas

Leisure

ESSENTIAL INFORMATION

- Finding the way to a place of entertainment, see p. 22.
- For times of day, see p. 127.
- Important signs, see p. 119.
- There are some resorts in Greece where you have to pay to go on the beach and to hire deckchairs and sunshades.
- Smoking is forbidden in cinemas and theatres, but not in open-air cinemas, open during the summer months.
- You should tip cinema and theatre usherettes who will also give you a programme.

WHAT TO SAY

At what time does . . . open?	Τί ὥρα ἀνοίγει . . .
	tee ora aneeg-ee . . .
the art gallery	ἡ πινακοθήκη;
	ee peenakoth-eekee
the cinema	τό σινεμά;
	toh seenema
the concert hall	ἡ αἴθουσα συναυλιῶν;
	ee eth-oossa seen-avlee-on
the disco	ἡ ντισκοτέκ;
	ee discotheque
the museum	τό μουσεῖο;
	toh moossee-o
the nightclub	τό νάιτ κλάμπ;
	toh nightclub
the sports stadium	τό γήπεδο;
	toh yee-petho
the swimming pool	ἡ πισίνα;
	ee pee-s-eena
the theatre	τό θέατρο;
	toh theh-atro
the zoo	ὁ ζωολογικός κῆπος;
	o zo-olog-eekoss keeposs
At what time does . . . close?	Τί ὥρα κλείνει . . .
	tee ora kleenee . . .
the art gallery	ἡ πινακοθήκη;
[see above list]	ee peenakoth-eekee

At what time does . . . start?	Τί ὥρα ἀρχίζει . . .
	tee ora ar-heezee . . .
the cabaret	τό καμπαρέ;
	toh cabaret
the concert	ἡ συναυλία;
	ee seen-avleea
the film	τό φίλμ;
	toh film
the match	τό μάτς;
	toh match
the play	τό θέατρο;
	toh theh-atro
the race	ὁ ἀγώνας;
	o agon-ass
How much is it . . .	Πόσο κάνει . . .
	posso kan-ee . . .
for an adult?	γιά τούς ἐνήλικες;
	ya tooss en-eeleek-ess
for a child?	γιά ἕνα παιδί;
	ya enna peth-ee
Two adults, please	Δύο ἐνήλικες, παρακαλῶ
	thee-o en-eeleek-ess parakalo
Three children, please	Τρία παιδιά, παρακαλῶ
[state price, if there's a choice]	tree-a peth-ya parakalo
Stalls/circle	Πλατεῖα/ἐξώστη
	plat-ee-a/ek-sostee
Do you have . . .	Ἔχετε . . .
	eh-het-eh. . .
a programme?	ἕνα πρόγραμμα;
	enna programma
a guide book?	ἕνα βιβλίο ὁδηγό;
	enna veevlee-o otheego
Where's the toilet please?	Ποῦ εἶναι ἡ τουαλέτα, παρακαλῶ;
	poo eeneh ee too-al-et-a parakalo
Where's the cloakroom?	Ποῦ εἶναι τό βεστιάριο;
	poo eeneh toh vestee-ario
I would like lessons in . . .	Θά ἤθελα μαθήματα . . .
	tha eeethella matheemata . . .
sailing	ἱστιοπλοΐας
	eestee-oplo-ee-ass
skiing	γιά σκί
	ya skee
sub-aqua diving	γιά ὑποβρύχιές βουτιές
	ya eepovree-hee-ess voot-ee-ess

I would like lessons in . . .	Θά ἤθελα μαθήματα . . .
	tha *eee*thella math*ee*mata . . .
water skiing	γιά θαλάσσιο σκί
	ya thal*a*ss-yo sk*ee*
windsurfing	σέ ουιντσέρφιγκ
	seh windsurfing
Can I hire . . .	Μπορῶ νά νοικιάσω . . .
	boro na neek-y*a*sso. . .
some skis	μερικά θαλάσσια σκί;
	mehr-eeka thal*a*ss-ya sk*ee*
a boat?	μία βάρκα;
	m*ee*-a varka
a fishing rod?	ἕνα καλάμι γιά ψάρεμα;
	*e*nna kalam-ee ya psarema
a deck-chair	μία ξαπλώστρα;
	m*ee*a ksap-lostra
a sun umbrella?	μία τέντα γιά τόν ἥλιο;
	m*ee*-a tenda ya ton *ee*l-yo
the necessary equipment?	τά ἀπαραίτητα ἐφόδια;
	ta aparet-eeta ef-*o*thee-a
How much is it . . .	Πόσο κάνει . . .
	p*o*sso kan-ee . . .
per day/per hour?	τῆ μέρα/τήν ὥρα;
	tee mehra/teen ora
Do I need a licence?	Χρειάζομαι ἄδεια;
	hree-*az*-om-eh *a*th-ia

Asking if things are allowed

WHAT TO SAY

Excuse me, please	Μέ συγχωρεῖτε, παρακαλῶ
	meh seenhoreet-eh parakalo
May one . . . here?	Ἐπιτρέπεται . . . ἐδῶ;
	epeetrep-et-eh . . . etho
camp	ἡ κατασκήνωση
	katass-keenoss-ee
fish	τό ψάρεμα
	toh psarem-ah
park	τό παρκάρισμα
	toh parkareesmah
smoke	τό κάπνισμα
	toh kapneesmah
swim	τό κολύμπι
	toh koleembeé
Can I . . .	Μπορῶ νά . . .
	bor-o na . . .
come in?	μπῶ ἐδῶ;
	boh etho
dance here?	χορέψω ἐδῶ;
	horepso etho
get a drink here?	πάρω ἕνα ποτό ἐδῶ;
	paro enna poto etho
get out this way?	βγῶ ἀπό ἐδῶ;
	vgoh apo etho
get something to eat here?	φάω ἐδῶ;
	fa-oh etho
leave my things here?	ἀφήσω τά πράγματα μου ἐδῶ;
	afeesso ta pragmata moo etho
look around?	ρίξω μία ματιά;
	reekso mee-a matya
sit here?	καθήσω ἐδῶ;
	katheesso etho
take photos here?	πάρω φωτογραφίες ἐδῶ;
	paro fotografeeyess etho
telephone here?	τηλεφωνήσω ἐδῶ;
	teelefoneessoh etho
wait here?	περιμένω ἐδῶ;
	pereemeno etho

LIKELY REACTIONS

Yes, certainly	Ναί, βεβαίως;
	neh vev-eh-oss
Help yourself	Βεβαίως
	vev-eh-oss
I think so	Μᾶλλον
	mallon
Of course	Φυσικά
	fee-seeka
Yes, but be careful	Ναί ἀλλά προσεκτικά
	neh alla pross-ek-teeka
No, certainly not	Ὄχι, δέν γίνεται
	o-hee then geenet-eh
I don't think so	Δέν νομίζω
	then nomeezo
Not normally	Συνήθως ὄχι
	seeneethoss o-hee
Sorry	Λυπᾶμαι
	leepam-eh

Reference

PUBLIC NOTICES

- Key words on signs for drivers, pedestrians, travellers, shoppers and overnight guests.

ΑΔΙΕΞΟΔΟΣ *athee-ek-sothoss*	Cul-de-sac
ΑΙΘΟΥΣΑ ΑΝΑΜΟΝΗΣ *ethoossa anamon-eess*	Waiting room
ΑΝΑΜΕΙΝΑΤΕ *anameenat-eh*	Wait
ΑΝΑΧΩΡΗΣΕΙΣ *ana-horeess-eess*	Departures
ΑΝΑΨΥΚΤΙΚΑ *an-apseekteek-a*	Refreshments
ΑΝΕΛΚΥΣΤΗΡ *an-elkeest-eer*	Lift
ΑΝΟΙΚΤΟΝ *an-eekton*	Open
ΑΝΔΡΩΝ *anthron*	Gentlemen
ΑΠΑΓΟΡΕΥΕΤΑΙ *apagorev-et-eh*	Forbidden
ΑΠΑΓΟΡΕΥΕΤΑΙ Η ΕΙΣΟΔΟΣ *apagorev-et-eh ee ees-othoss*	No entry
ΑΠΑΓΟΡΕΥΕΤΑΙ Η ΣΤΑΘΜΕΥΣΙΣ *apagorev-et-eh ee stathmef-seess*	No parking
ΑΠΑΓΟΡΕΥΕΤΑΙ ΤΟ ΚΑΠΝΙΣΜΑ *apagorev-et-eh toh kapnizma*	No smoking
ΑΠΩΛΕΣΘΕΝΤΑ ΑΝΤΙΚΕΙΜΕΝΑ *ap-ol-ess-thenda antik-eemena*	Lost property
ΑΡΓΑ *arga*	Drive slowly
ΑΣΤΥΝΟΜΙΑ *asteen-omee-a*	Police

ΑΦΙΞΕΙΣ	Arrivals
afeek-seess	
ΒΑΓΚΟΝ-ΡΕΣΤΩΡΑΝ	Dining car
vagon restoran	
ΓΡΑΦΕΙΟΝ ΕΚΔΟΣΕΩΣ ΕΙΣΙΤΗΡΙΩΝ	Ticket office
grafee-on ek-thoss-eh-oss eess-eeteer-ee-on	
ΓΡΑΦΕΙΟΝ ΠΛΗΡΟΦΟΡΙΩΝ	Information office
grafee-on pleer-oforee-on	
ΓΥΝΑΙΚΩΝ	Ladies
gheenek-on	
ΔΙΑΣΤΑΥΡΩΣΙΣ	Crossroads
thee-astavross-eess	
ΔΙΑ ΦΟΡΤΗΓΑ ΑΥΤΟΚΙΝΗΤΑ	For heavy vehicles
thee-a fort-eega aftokeen-eeta	
ΔΙΟΔΙΑ	Toll
thee-oth-ya	
ΕΘΝΙΚΗ ΟΔΟΣ	Motorway
ethneekee othoss	
ΕΙΔΙΚΗ ΠΡΟΣΦΟΡΑ	Special offer
ee-theekee prosfora	
ΕΙΣΟΔΟΣ	Entrance
eess-othoss	
ΕΙΣΟΔΟΣ ΕΛΕΥΘΕΡΑ	Admission free
eess-othoss el-ef-thehra	
ΕΙΣΟΔΟΣ ΕΛΕΥΘΕΡΑ	Entrance free
eess-oth-oss el-ef-thehra	
ΕΚΠΤΩΣΕΙΣ	Sales
ek-ptoss-eess	
ΕΛΑΤΤΩΣΑΤΕ ΤΑΧΥΤΗΤΑ	Slow down
el-atossat-eh ta-heeteeta	
ΕΛΕΥΘΕΡΟΝ	Vacant
el-ef-thehron	
ΕΝΟΙΚΙΑΖΕΤΑΙ	For hire
en-eek-yaz-et-eh	
ΕΝΟΙΚΙΑΖΕΤΑΙ	To let
en-eek-yaz-et-eh	
ΕΝΟΙΚΙΑΖΟΝΤΑΙ ΔΩΜΑΤΙΑ	Room to let
eneekeeazondeh thomatee-a	
ΕΞΟΔΟΣ	Exit
ek-sothoss	

ΙΣΟΠΕΔΟΣ ΔΙΑΒΑΣΙΣ eessopethoss thee-avass-eess	Level crossing
ΕΡΓΑ ΕΠΙ ΤΗΣ ΟΔΟΥ ehr-ga ep-ee teess othoo	Road works
ΕΞΟΔΟΣ ΚΙΝΔΥΝΟΥ ek-sothoss kintheenoo	Emergency exit
ΖΕΣΤΟ zesto	Hot (tap)
ΘΥΡΙΔΕΣ ΑΠΟΣΚΕΥΩΝ theer-eethess aposkev-on	Left luggage
ΙΔΙΩΤΙΚΟΝ ee-thee-oteekon	Private
ΚΑΤΕΙΛΗΜΜΕΝΟΝ kat-eeleemmen-on	Engaged/Occupied
ΚΙΝΔΥΝΟΣ kinth-inoss	Danger
ΚΛΕΙΣΤΟΝ kleeston	Closed
ΚΡΥΟ kree-o	Cold
ΚΥΛΙΟΜΕΝΗ ΣΚΑΛΑ keel-yom-en-ee ska-la	Escalator
ΜΗ ΕΓΓΙΖΕΤΕ mee eng-eezet-eh	Do not touch
ΜΗ ΠΟΣΙΜΟ ΝΕΡΟ mee posseemo nehr-o	Not for drinking
ΜΟΝΟΔΡΟΜΟΣ monoth-romoss	One-way (street)
ΜΠΑΡ bar	Bar
ΝΟΣΟΚΟΜΕΙΟΝ noss-okomee-on	Hospital
ΟΔΗΓΟΣ othee-goss	Guide
ΟΙ ΠΑΡΑΒΑΤΑΙ ΘΑ ΔΙΩΧΘΟΥΝ ee paravat-eh tha thee-o-hthoon	Trespassers will be prosecuted
ΟΛΙΣΘΗΡΗ ΕΠΙΦΑΝΕΙΑ ol-eess-theeree ep-eefan-ya	Slippery surface (road)
ΟΡΙΟΝ ΤΑΧΥΤΗΤΟΣ oree-on ta-heeteetoss	Speed limit

ΟΡΟΦΟΣ (ΠΡΩΤΟΣ, ΔΕΥΤΕΡΟΣ, ΤΡΙΤΟΣ, ΕΙΣΟΓΕΙΟΝ, ΥΠΟΓΕΙΟΝ) orofoss (prot-oss, thefteross, treetoss, eessog-yon, eepog-yon)	Floor (first, second, third ground, basement)
ΠΕΖΟΙ pez-ee	Pedestrians
ΠΕΡΙΟΡΙΣΜΕΝΗ ΣΤΑΘΜΕΥΣΙΣ peri-oreezmen-ee stathmef-seess	Restricted parking
ΠΛΑΤΦΟΡΜΑ platforma	Platform
ΠΛΗΡΕΣ pleeress	No vacancies
ΠΟΡΕΙΑ ΥΠΟΧΡΕΩΤΙΚΗ ΔΕΞΙΑ poree-a eepo-hreh-oteekee theks-ya	Keep right
ΠΟΣΙΜΟ ΝΕΡΟ posseemo nehro	Drinking water
ΠΡΟΣΟΧΗ prosso-hee	Caution
ΠΡΟΣΟΧΗ ΣΚΥΛΟΣ prosso-hee skeeloss	Beware of the dog
ΠΡΟΣΟΧΗ ΣΤΑ ΤΡΑΙΝΑ prosso-hee sta tren-a	Beware of the trains
ΠΩΛΕΙΤΑΙ poleeteh	For sale
ΠΩΛΗΣΙΣ pol-eess-eess	Sale
ΡΕΣΕΠΣΙΟΝ ressepsee-on	Reception
ΣΕΛΦ-ΣΕΡΒΙΣ self-service	Self-service
ΣΤΑΘΜΕΥΣΙΣ ΑΥΤΟΚΙΝΗΤΩΝ stathmef-seess aftokeen-eeton	Car park
ΣΥΡΑΤΕ seerat-eh	Push

ΣΧΟΛΕΙΟΝ skol*ee*-on	School
ΤΑΜΕΙΟΝ tam-*ee*-on	Cash desk
ΤΕΛΩΝΕΙΟΝ tel-on*ee*-on	Customs
ΤΟΥΑΛΕΤΑ too-al-*et*-a	Bathroom
ΤΡΑΠΕΖΑΡΙΑ trap-ez-ar*ee*-a	Dining room
ΦΑΝΑΡΙΑ fan*ar*-ee-a	Traffic lights
ΩΘΗΣΑΤΕ oth*ee*-sat-eh	Pull

ABBREVIATIONS

Ἅγ.	Ἅγιος	Saint
ΑΠ	Ἀστυνομία Πόλεων	Municipal Police
ἀρ.	ἀριθμός	street number
ΔΕΗ	Δημόσια Ἐπιχείρησις Ἠλεκτρισμοῦ	Electric Company of Greece
δηλ.	δηλαδή	that is to say
Δίς	Δεσποινίς	Miss
δολλ.	δολλάρια	dollars
δρχ.	δραχμές	drachmas
Δσις	Διεύθυνσις	manager
ΕΕΣ	Ἑλληνικός Ἐρυθρός Σταυρός	Greek Red Cross
ἐθν.	ἐθνικός	national
ἐκ.	ἑκατοστά	centimetres
	ἑκατομμύρια	millions
Ἑλλ.	Ἑλληνικός	Greek
ΕΛΠΑ	Ἑλληνική Λέσχη Περιηγήσεων καί Αὐτοκινήτου	Automobile and Touring Club of Greece
ΕΛ.ΤΑ.	Ἑλληνικά Ταχυδρομεῖα	Greek Post Office
ΕΟΤ	Ἑλληνικός Ὀργανισμός Τουρισμοῦ	Greek Tourist Organization
ΙΚΑ	Ἵδρυμα Κοινωνικῶν Ἀσφαλίσεων	National Health Insurance
Κ./Κος	Κύριος	Mr
Κα	Κυρία	Mrs
κλπ.	καί τά λοιπά	etc.
Λεωφ.	Λεωφόρος	avenue
λογ/μος	λογαριασμός	bill
λ.στ.	λίραι στερλίναι ·	sterling pounds
μ.μ.	μετά μεσημβρίαν	p.m.
μ.Χ.	μετά Χριστόν	AD
Ὁδ.	Ὁδός	street
ΟΣΕ	Ὀργανισμός Σιδηροδρόμων Ἑλλάδος	Railway Company of Greece
ΟΤΕ	Ὀργανισμός Τηλεπικοινωνιῶν Ἑλλάδος	Telecommunications Company of Greece
π.μ.	πρό μεσημβρίας	a.m.
π.Χ.	· πρό Χριστοῦ	BC
π.χ.	παραδείγματος χάριν	for example
ΤΑ ·	Τουριστική Ἀστυνομία	Tourist Police
τηλ.	τηλέφωνο	telephone
χλμ.	χιλιόμετρα ·	kilometres

NUMBERS

Cardinal numbers

0	μηδέν	meethen
1	ἕνας, μία, ἕνα	ennas mee-a enna
2	δύο	thee-o
3	τρία	tree-a
4	τέσσερα	tessera
5	πέντε	pendeh
6	ἕξη	eksee
7	ἑπτά	epta
8	ὀκτώ	okto
9	ἐννέα	enneh-a
10	δέκα	theh-ka
11	ἕντεκα	endek-a
12	δώδεκα	thothek-a
13	δεκατρία	thek-atree-a
14	δεκατέσσερα	thek-atesser-a
15	δεκαπέντε	thek-apendeh
16	δεκαέξη	theh-ka-eksee
17	δεκαεπτά	theh-ka-ept-a
18	δεκαοκτώ	theh-ka-okto
19	δεκαεννέα	theh-ka-enneh-a
20	εἴκοσι	eekossee
21	εἴκοσι ἕνα	eekossee enna
22	εἴκοσι δύο	eekossee thee-o
23	εἴκοσι τρία	eekossee tree-a
24	εἴκοσι τέσσερα	eekossee tessera
25	εἴκοσι πέντε	eekossee pendeh
26	εἴκοσι ἕξη	eekossee eksee
27	εἴκοσι ἑπτά	eekossee epta
28	εἴκοσι ὀκτώ	eekossee okto
29	εἴκοσι ἐννέα	eekossee enneh-a
30	τριάντα	tree-anda
35	τριάντα πέντε	tree-anda pendeh
38	τριάντα ὀκτώ	tree-anda okto
40	σαράντα	saranda
41	σαράντα ἕνα	saranda enna
45	σαράντα πέντε	saranda pendeh
48	σαράντα ὀκτώ	saranda okto
50	πενήντα	pen-eenda
55	πενήντα πέντε	pen-eenda pendeh
56	πενήντα ἕξη	pen-eenda eksee

60	ἑξήντα	ekseenda
65	ἑξήντα πέντε	ekseenda pendeh
70	ἑβδομῆντα	ev-thomeenda
75	ἑβδομῆντα πέντε	ev-thomeenda pendeh
80	ὀγδόντα	ogthonda
85	ὀγδόντα πέντε	ogthonda pendeh
90	ἐνενῆντα	enneh-neenda
95	ἐνενῆντα πέντε	enneh-neenda pendeh
100	ἑκατό	ek-at-o
101	ἑκατόν ἕνα	ek-at-on enna
102	ἑκατόν δύο	ek-at-on thee-o
125	ἑκατόν εἴκοσι πέντε	ek-at-on eekossee pendeh
150	ἑκατόν πενῆντα	ek-at-on pen-eenda
175	ἑκατόν ἑβδομῆντα πέντε	ek-at-on ev-thomeenda pendeh
200	διακόσια	thee-akoss-ya
300	τριακόσια	tree-akoss-ya
400	τετρακόσια	tetra-koss-ya
500	πεντακόσια	pend-akoss-ya
1,000	χίλια	heel-ya
1,500	χίλια πεντακόσια	heel-ya pend-akoss-ya
2,000	δύο χιλιάδες	thee-o heel-yathess
5,000	πέντε χιλιάδες	pendeh heel-yathess
10,000	δέκα χιλιάδες	theh-ka heel-yathess
100,000	ἑκατόν χιλιάδες	ek-at-on heel-yathess
1,000,000	ἕνα ἑκατομμύριο	enna ekatomeereeo

Ordinal numbers

1st	πρῶτος, πρώτη, πρῶτο (1ος)	prot-oss prot-ee prot-o
2nd	δεύτερος (2ος)	thefteross
3rd	τρίτος (3ος)	treetoss
4th	τέταρτος (4ος)	tet-artoss
5th	πέμπτος (5ος)	pemp-toss
6th	ἕκτος (6ος)	ektoss
7th	ἕβδομος (7ος)	ev-thom-oss
8th	ὄγδοος (8ος)	ogtho-oss
9th	ἔννατος (9ος)	ennat-oss
10th	δέκατος (10ος)	thek-at-oss
11th	ἐντέκατος (11ος)	endeka-toss
12th	δωδέκατος (12ος)	tho-theka-toss

TIME

What time is it?	Τί ὥρα εἶναι;
	tee ora eeneh
It's ...	Εἶναι ...
	eeneh ...
one o'clock	μία
	mee-a
two o'clock	δύο
	thee-o
three o'clock	τρεῖς
	treess
four o'clock	τέσσερες
	tesser-ess
in the morning	τό πρωί
	toh pro-ee
in the afternoon	τό ἀπόγευμα
	toh apog-evma
in the evening	τό βράδυ
	toh vrath-ee
at night	τή νύχτα
	tee neeh-tah
It's ...	Εἶναι ...
	eeneh ...
noon	μεσημέρι
	mess-eemehree
midnight	μεσάνυχτα
	messan-ee-hta
It's ...	Εἶναι ...
	eeneh ...
five past five	πέντε καί πέντε
	pendeh keh pendeh
ten past five	πέντε καί δέκα
	pendeh keh theh-ka
a quarter past five	πέντε καί τέταρτο
	pendeh keh tet-arto·
twenty past five	πέντε καί εἴκοσι
	pendeh keh eekossee
twenty-five past five	πέντε καί εἴκοσι πέντε
	pendeh keh eekossee pendeh
half past five	πέντε καί μισή
	pendeh keh meessee

It's . . .	Εἶναι . . .
	eeneh . . .
twenty-five to six	ἕξη παρά εἴκοσι πέντε
	eksee para eekossee pendeh
twenty to six	ἕξη παρά εἴκοσι
	eksee para eekossee
a quarter to six	ἕξη παρά τέταρτο
	eksee para tet-arto
ten to six	ἕξη παρά δέκα
	eksee para theh-ka
five to six	ἕξη παρά πέντε
	eksee para pendeh
At what time . . . (does the train leave)?	Τί ὥρα (φεύγει τό τραῖνο);
	tee ora (fev-ghee toh tren-o)
At . . .	Στίς . . .
	steess . . .
13.00	δέκα τρεῖς
	theh-ka treess
14.05	δέκα τέσσερες καί πέντε
	theh-ka tesser-ess keh pendeh
15.10	δέκα πέντε καί δέκα
	theh-ka pendeh keh theh-ka
16.15	δέκα ἕξη καί δέκα πέντε
	theh-ka eksee keh theh-ka pendeh
17.20	δέκα ἑπτά καί εἴκοσι
	theh-ka epta keh eekossee
18.25	δέκα ὀκτώ καί εἴκοσι πέντε
	theh-ka okto keh eekossee pendeh
19.30	δέκα ἐννέα καί τριάντα
	theh-ka ennea keh tree-and-a
20.35	εἴκοσι καί τριάντα πέντε
	eekossee keh tree-anda pendeh
21.40	εἴκοσι μία καί σαράντα
	eekossee mee-a keh saranda
22.45	εἴκοσι δύο καί σαράντα πέντε
	eekossee thee-o keh saranda pendeh
23.50	εἴκοσι τρεῖς καί πενῆντα
	eekossee treess keh pen-eenda
00.55	δώδεκα καί πενῆντα πέντε
	thoth-eka keh pen-eenda pendeh
in ten minutes	σέ δέκα λεπτά
	seh theh-ka lepta

in a quarter of an hour	σέ ἕνα τέταρτο
	seh enna tet-arto
in half an hour	σέ μισή ὥρα
	seh meessee ora
in three quarters of an hour	σέ τρία τέταρτα
	seh tree-a tet-arta

DAYS

Monday	Δευτέρα
	thef-tehra
Tuesday	Τρίτη
	treetee
Wednesday	Τετάρτη
	tet-artee
Thursday	Πέμπτη
	pemp-tee
Friday	Παρασκευή
	paraskev-ee
Saturday	Σάββατο
	savvato
Sunday	Κυριακή
	keeree-ak-ee
last Monday	τήν προηγούμενη Δευτέρα
	teen pro-eegoomen-ee thef-tehra
next Tuesday	τήν ἑπόμενη Τρίτη
	teen ep-om-en-ee treetee
on Wednesday	τήν Τετάρτη
	teen tet-artee
on Thursdays	κάθε Πέμπτη
	kath-eh pemp-tee
until Friday	μέχρι τήν Παρασκευή
	meh-hree teen paraskev-ee
before Saturday	πρίν τό Σάββατο
	preen toh savvato
after Sunday	μετά τήν Κυριακή
	meta teen keeree-ak-ee
the day before yesterday	προχθές
	pro-hthess
two days ago	πρίν δύο μέρες
	preen thee-o mehr-ess
yesterday	χθές
	hthess

yesterday morning	χθές τό πρωί
	hthess toh pro-*ee*
yesterday afternoon	χθές τό ἀπόγευμα
	hthess toh ap*og*-evma
last night	χθές τό βράδυ
	hthess toh v*r*ath-ee
today	σήμερα
	s*ee*mera
this morning	τό πρωί
	toh pro-*ee*
this afternoon	τό ἀπόγευμα
	toh ap*og*-evma
tonight	τό βράδυ
	toh v*r*ath-ee
tomorrow	αὔριο
	*a*vrio
tomorrow morning	αὔριο τό πρωί
	*a*vrio toh pro-*ee*
tomorrow afternoon	αὔριο τό ἀπόγευμα
	*a*vrio toh ap*og*-evma
tomorrow evening	αὔριο βράδυ
	*a*vrio vrath-ee
tomorrow night	αὔριο βράδυ
	*a*vrio vrath-ee
the day after tomorrow	μεθαύριο ··
	meth*a*vrio

MONTHS AND DATES

January	'Ιανουάριος yanoo-*ar*-ee-oss
February	Φεβρουάριος fevroo-*ar*-ee-oss
March	Μάρτιος *martee*-oss
April	'Απρίλιος ap*reelee*-oss
May	Μάϊος ma-ee-oss
June	'Ιούνιος ee-*oo*nee-oss
July	'Ιούλιος ee-*oo*lee-oss
August	Αὔγουστος *avgoost*-oss
September	Σεπτέμβριος septem-*vree*-oss
October	'Οκτώβριος okt*ovree*-oss
November	Νοέμβριος no-*em*-vree-oss
December	Δεκέμβριος thek-*em*-vree-oss
in January	τόν 'Ιανουάριο ton yanoo-*ar*-ee-o
until February	μέχρι τόν φεβρουάριο meh-hree ton fev-roo-*ar*-ee-o
before March	πρίν τόν Μάρτιο preen ton *martee*-o
after April	μετά τόν 'Απρίλιο met-*a* ton ap*reelee*-o
during May	κατά τήν διάρκεια τοῦ Μαΐου kata teen thee-*ark*-ya too ma-*ee*-oo
not until June	ὄχι πρίν τόν 'Ιούνιο o-hee preen ton ee-*oo*nee-o
the beginning of July	ἀρχές 'Ιουλίου ar-hess ee-*oolee*-oo
the middle of August	μέσα Αὐγούστου messa avg*oost*-oo

the end of September	τέλη Σεπτεμβρίου
	tel-ee septem-vree-oo
last month	τόν προηγούμενο μῆνα
	ton pro-eegoomen-o meena
this month	αὐτό τό μῆνα
	afto toh meena
next month	τόν ἑπόμενο μῆνα
	ton ep-om-en-o meena
in spring	τήν ἄνοιξη
	teen an-eeksee
in summer	τό καλοκαίρι
	toh kalok-ehree
in autumn	τό φθινόπωρο
	toh ftheen-op-oro
in winter	τό χειμῶνα
	toh heemona
this year	αὐτό τό χρόνο
	afto toh hron-o
last year	πέρυσι
	pehr-eessee
next year	τοῦ χρόνου
	too hron-oo
in 1983	τό χίλια ἐννιακόσια ὀγδόντα τρία
	toh heel-ya enneh-akoss-ya ogthonda tree-a
in 1985	τό χίλια ἐννιακόσια ὀγδόντα πέντε
	toh heel-ya enneh-akoss-ya ogthonda pendeh
in 1990	τό χίλια ἐννιακόσια ἐνενήντα
	toh heel-ya enneh-akoss-ya ennen-eenda
What's the date today?	Πόσο ἔχει ὁ μήνας σήμερα;
	posso eh-hee o meen-ass seemera
It's the 6th of March	Εἶναι ἕξη Μαρτίου
	eeneh eksee martee-oo
It's the 12th April	Εἶναι δώδεκα ᾽Απριλίου
	eeneh thoth-eka apreelee-oo
It's the 21st of August	Εἶναι εἴκοσι μία Αὐγούστου
	eeneh eekossee mee-a avgoost-oo

Public holidays

● On these days offices, shops and schools are closed:

1 January	Πρωτοχρονιά	New Year's Day
6 January	Ἐπιφάνεια	Epiphany
	⌈ Καθαρή Δευτέρα	Clean Monday: beginning of Lent
moveable dates	Μεγάλη Παρασκευή	Good Friday
	Δεύτερη μέρα τοῦ Πάσχα	Easter Monday
	⌊ Πεντηκοστή	Whit Monday
25 March	25 Μαρτίου	Independence Day
1 May	Πρωτομαγιά	May Day
15 August	15 Αὐγούστου	Assumption
28 October	28 Ὀκτωβρίου	Ochi Day
25 December	Χριστούγεννα	Christmas Day
26 December	Δεύτερη μέρα τῶν Χριστουγέννων	Boxing Day

COUNTRIES AND NATIONALITIES
Countries

Australia	Αὐστραλία
	afstralee-a
for Australia	Γιά τήν Αὐστραλία
	ya teen afstralee-a
to Australia	Στήν Αὐστραλία
	steen afstralee-a
Austria	Αὐστρία
	afstree-a
Belgium	Βέλγιο
	velg-yo
for Belgium	Γιά τό Βέλγιο
	ya toh velg-yo
to Belgium	Στό Βέλγιο
	sto velg-yo
Britain	Βρεταννία
	vret-annee-a
Canada	Καναδᾶς
	kana-thass
for Canada	Γιά τόν Καναδᾶ
	ya ton kana-tha
to Canada	Στόν Καναδᾶ
	ston kana-tha
East African	Ἀνατολική Ἀφρική
	anatoleekee afreekee
Eire	Ἰρλανδία
	eerlan-thee-a
England	Ἀγγλία
	anglee-a
France	Γαλλία
	gall-eea
Greece	Ἑλλάδα
	ellatha
India	Ἰνδία
	een-thee-a
Italy	Ἰταλία
	eetal-ee-a
Luxembourg	Λουξεμβοῦργο
	looksemvoorgo

Netherlands	Ὀλλανδία
	ollan-th*ee*-a
New Zealand	Νέα Ζηλανδία
	neh-a zeelan-th*ee*-a
Northern Ireland	Βόρειος Ἰρλανδία
	v*o*ree-oss eerlan-th*ee*-a
Pakistan	Πακιστάν
	pakist*a*n
Portugal	Πορτογαλία
	portogal-*ee*-a
Scotland	Σκωτία
	skot-*ee*-a
South African	Νότιος Ἀφρική
	n*o*tee-oss afreek*ee*
Spain	Ἰσπανία
	eespan-*ee*-a
Switzerland	Ἐλβετία
	elvet-*ee*-a
United States	Οἱ Ἡνωμένες Πολιτεῖες
	ee eenom*e*n-ess poleet*ee*-ess
Wales	Οὐαλλία
	oo-al-l*ee*-a
West Germany	Δυτική Γερμανία
	theeteek-*ee* yehr-man*ee*-a
West Indies	Οἱ Δυτικές Ἰνδίες
	ee theeteek-*ess* een-th*ee*-ess
for the West Indies	Γιά τίς Δυτικές Ἰνδίες
	ya teess theeteek-*ess* een-th*ee*-ess
to the West Indies	Στίς Δυτικές Ἰνδίες
	steess theeteek-*ess* een-th*ee*-ess

Nationalities
(Use the first alternative for men, the second for women)

American	'Αμερικανός/'Αμερικανίδα
	amerikan-oss/amerikan-eetha
Australian	Αὐστραλός/Αὐστραλέζα
	afstral-oss/afstral-ez-a
British	Βρεταννός/Βρεταννίδα
	vretann-oss/vrettan-eetha
Canadian	Καναδός/Καναδέζα
	kanath-oss/kanathez-a
East African	ἀπό τήν 'Ανατολική 'Αφρική
	apo teen anatoleekee afreekee
English	'Εγγλέζος/'Εγγλέζα
	englez-oss/englez-a
Indian	'Ινδός/'Ινδή
	eenthoss/eenthee
Irish	'Ιρλανδός/'Ιρλανδή
	eerlan-thoss/eerlan-thee
a New Zealander	Νέο Ζηλανδός/Νέο Ζηλανδή
	neh-ozeelan-thoss/neh-ozeelan-thee
a Pakistani	Πακιστανός/Πακιστανή
	pakistan-oss/pakistan-ee
Scots	Σκωτσέζος/Σκωτσέζα
	skotsez-oss/skotsez-a
South African	ἀπό τήν Νότια 'Αφρική
	apo teen notee-a afreekee
Welsh	Οὐαλλός/Οὐαλλή
	oo-al-loss/oo-al-lee
West Indian	ἀπό τίς Δυτικές 'Ινδίες
	apo teess theeteek-ess eenthee-ess

DEPARTMENT STORE GUIDE

ΑΝΔΡΙΚΑ ΕΙΔΗ	Menswear
ΑΝΔΡΙΚΑ ΕΣΩΡΟΥΧΑ	Underclothes
ΑΡΩΜΑΤΟΠΩΛΕΙΟΝ	Perfumery
ΓΡΑΒΑΤΕΣ	Ties
ΓΥΝΑΙΚΕΙΑ ΕΙΔΗ	Ladies' fashion
ΓΥΝΑΙΚΕΙΑ ΕΣΩΡΟΥΧΑ	Lingerie
ΓΥΝΑΙΚΕΙΙΑ ΕΣΩΡΟΥΧΑ	Underwear (women)
ΔΕΡΜΑΤΙΝΑ ΕΙΔΗ	Leather goods
ΔΕΥΤΕΡΟΣ	Second
ΔΙΣΚΟΙ	Records
ΔΩΡΑ	Presents
ΕΙΔΗ ΚΑΘΑΡΙΣΜΟΥ	Cleaning material
ΕΙΔΗ ΚΑΤΑΣΚΗΝΩΣΕΩΣ	Camping
ΕΙΔΗ ΚΡΕΒΒΑΤΟΚΑΜΑΡΑΣ	Bedding
ΕΙΔΗ ΡΑΠΤΙΚΗΣ	Haberdashery
ΕΠΙΠΛΑ	Furniture
ΕΠΙΠΛΑ ΚΟΥΖΙΝΑΣ	Kitchen furniture
ΕΤΟΙΜΑ ΕΝΔΥΜΑΤΑ	Ready made clothing
ΖΩΝΕΣ	Belts
ΗΛΕΚΤΡΙΚΑ ΕΙΔΗ	Electrical appliances
ΚΑΛΛΥΝΤΙΚΑ	Cosmetics
ΚΑΛΤΣΕΣ	Stockings
ΚΟΣΜΗΜΑΤΑ	Jewellery
ΚΟΥΒΕΡΤΕΣ	Blankets
ΚΟΥΡΤΙΝΕΣ	Curtains
ΜΑΞΙΛΑΡΙΑ	Cushions
ΜΠΛΟΥΖΕΣ	Blouses
ΟΡΟΦΟΣ	Floor
ΠΑΙΔΙΚΑ	Children
ΠΑΙΧΝΙΔΙΑ	Toys
ΠΑΝΤΟΦΛΕΣ	Slippers
ΠΗΛΙΝΑ ΕΙΔΗ	Earthenware
ΠΗΛΙΝΑ ΣΚΕΥΗ	Crockery
ΠΛΗΡΟΦΟΡΙΕΣ	Information
ΠΟΡΣΕΛΛΑΝΕΣ	China
ΠΟΥΛΟΒΕΡ	Pullovers
ΠΡΩΤΟΣ	First
ΛΕΥΚΑ ΕΙΔΗ	Linen
ΣΙΔΗΡΙΚΑ	Hardware
ΣΤΗΘΟΔΕΣΜΟΙ	Bras

ΤΑΜΕΙΟΝ	Accounts
ΤΑΞΕΙΔΙΩΤΙΚΑ ΕΙΔΗ	Travel articles
ΤΑΠΕΤΣΑΡΙΑΙ	Furnishing fabrics
ΤΕΤΑΡΤΟΣ	Fourth
ΤΡΙΤΟΣ	Third
ΤΡΟΦΙΜΑ	Food
ΥΑΛΙΚΑ ΕΙΔΗ	Glassware
ΥΠΟΓΕΙΟΝ	Basement
ΥΠΟΚΑΜΙΣΑ	Shirts
ΥΦΑΣΜΑΤΑ	Drapery
ΦΩΤΟΓΡΑΦΙΚΑ ΕΙΔΗ	Photography
ΧΑΛΙΑ	Carpets
ΧΑΡΤΙΚΑ	Stationery

CONVERSION TABLES

Read the centre column of these tables from right to left to convert from metric to imperial and from left to right to convert from imperial to metric e.g. 5 litres = 8.80 pints; 5 pints = 2.84 litres

pints		litres		gallons		litres
1.76	1	0.57		0.22	1	4.55
3.52	2	1.14		0.44	2	9.09
5.28	3	1.70		0.66	3	13.64
7.07	4	2.27		0.88	4	18.18
8.80	5	2.84		1.00	5	22.73
10.56	6	3.41		1.32	6	27.28
12.32	7	3.98		1.54	7	31.82
14.08	8	4.55		1.76	8	36.37
15.84	9	5.11		1.98	9	40.91

ounces		grams		pounds		kilos
0.04	1	28.35		2.20	1	0.45
0.07	2	56.70		4.41	2	0.91
0.11	3	85.05		6.61	3	1.36
0.14	4	113.40		8.82	4	1.81
0.18	5	141.75		11.02	5	2.27
0.21	6	170.10		13.23	6	2.72
0.25	7	198.45		15.43	7	3.18
0.28	8	226.80		17.64	8	3.63
0.32	9	255.15		19.84	9	4.08

inches		centimetres		yards		metres
0.39	1	2.54		1.09	1	0.91
0.79	2	5.08		2.19	2	1.83
1.18	3	7.62		3.28	3	2.74
1.58	4	10.16		4.37	4	3.66
1.95	5	12.70		5.47	5	4.57
2.36	6	15.24		6.56	6	5.49
2.76	7	17.78		7.66	7	6.40
3.15	8	20.32		8.65	8	7.32
3.54	9	22.86		9.84	9	8.23

miles		kilometres
0.62	1	1.61
1.24	2	3.22
1.86	3	4.83
2.49	4	6.44
3.11	5	8.05
3.73	6	9.66
4.35	7	11.27
4.97	8	12.87
5.59	9	14.48

A quick way to convert kilometres to miles: divide by 8 and multiply by 5. To convert miles to kilometres: divide by 5 and multiply by 8.

fahrenheit (°F)	centigrade (°C)	lbs/ sq in	k/ sq cm
212°	100° boiling point	18	1.3
100°	38°	20	1.4
98.4°	36.9° body temperature	22	1.5
86°	30°	25	1.7
77°	25°	29	2.0
68°	20°	32	2.3
59°	15°	35	2.5
50°	10°	36	2.5
41°	5°	39	2.7
32°	0° freezing point	40	2.8
14°	−10°	43	3.0
−4°	−20°	45	3.2
		46	3.2
		50	3.5
		60	4.2

To convert °C to °F, divide by 5, multiply by 9 and add 32. To convert °F to °C, take away 32, divide by 9 and multiply by 5.

CLOTHING SIZES

Remember – always try on clothes before buying. Clothing sizes are usually unreliable.

Women's dresses and suits

Europe	38	40	42	44	46	48
UK	32	34	36	38	40	42
USA	10	12	14	16	18	20

Men's suits and coats

Europe	46	48	50	52	54	56
UK and USA	36	38	40	42	44	46

Men's shirts

Europe	36	37	38	39	41	42	43
UK and USA	14	14½	15	15½	16	16½	17

Socks

Europe	38–39	39–40	40–41	41–42	42–43
UK and USA	9½	10	10½	11	11½

Shoes

Europe	34	35½	36½	38	39	41	42	43	44	45
UK	2	3	4	5	6	7	8	9	10	11
USA	3½	4½	5½	6½	7½	8½	9½	10½	11½	12½

Do it yourself

Some notes on the language

This section does not deal with 'grammar' as such. The purpose here is to explain some of the most obvious and elementary nuts and bolts of the language, based on the principle phrases included in the book. This information should enable you to produce numerous sentences of your own making, although you will obviously still be fairly limited in what you can say.

THE

All nouns in Greek belong to one of three genders: masculine, feminine or neuter; this includes inanimate objects as well as living beings (see table opposite).

Important things to remember

- In the word list, *the* in the singular is:
  ὁ (o) before masculine nouns
  ἡ (ee) before feminine nouns
  τό (toh) before neuter nouns
- You can often tell if a noun is masculine, feminine or neuter by its ending. Most masculine nouns in the singular end in -ος (oss). Some end in -ας (ass) or ης (eess) but there are few examples in the phrase book. Most feminine nouns in -η (ee) or -α (ah) and most neuter nouns in -ο (oh), or ι (ee). If you are reading a word with ὁ (o), ἡ (ee), τό (toh) in front of it, you can detect its gender immediately: ὁ κατάλογος (o katalogoss) is masculine (m. in dictionaries), ἡ βαλίτσα (ee valeetsa) is feminine (f. in dictionaries) and τό δωμάτιο (toh thomateeo) is neuter (n. in dictionaries).
- Does it matter? Not unless you want to make a serious attempt to speak correctly and scratch beneath the surface of the language. You would be understood, if you said ἡ κατάλογος (ee katalogoss) or ὁ δρομολόγιο (o thromologeeo) providing your pronunciation was reasonable and you stressed the word in the right place.

The (singular)	masculine	feminine	neuter
the address		ἡ διεύθυνση ee thee- eftheensee	
the apple			τό μῆλο toh meeloh
the bill	ὁ λογαριασμός o logareeasmoss		
the cup of tea			τό τσάι toh tsaee
the glass of beer		ἡ μπύρα ee beera	
the key			τό κλειδί toh kleethee
the menu	ὁ κατάλογος o katalogoss		
the newspaper		ἡ 'εφημερίδα ee efeemereetha	
the receipt		ἡ ἀπόδειξη ee apotheeksee	
the sandwich			τό σάντουϊτς toh sandwich
the suitcase		ἡ βαλίτσα ee valeetsa	

the telephone
  directory
	ὁ τηλεφωνικός
	  κατάλογος
	o teelefoneekoss
	  katalogoss		

the timetable			τό δρομολόγιο toh thromologeeo

In phrases beginning: 'Have you got the . . .?'
                                 'I'd like the . . .?'
                                 'Where can I get the . . .?'
Greek nouns and articles become the object of the sentence and
change to form the accusative. In the singular that means:

	the	noun endings
masculine	ὁ (o) becomes τό (toh)	-ος (oss) becomes -ο (oh)
feminine	ἡ (ee) becomes τή (tee)	no change
neuter	no change	no change

e.g. ὁ κατάλογος (o katalogoss) becomes τό κατάλογο (toh katalogo)
and ἡ βαλίτσα (ee valeetsa) becomes τή βαλίτσα (tee valeetsa).

Practise saying and writing these sentences in Greek (masculine
nouns are marked * to remind you that *both* the article and the noun
ending change, but remember to change the article with feminine
nouns). When you have understood the sentences, we suggest that
you cover up the Greek and try yourself to work out translations.

Have you got the suitcase?	Ἔχετε τή βαλίτσα;
	eheteh tee valeetsa
Have you got the key?.	Ἔχετε τό κλειδί
	eheteh toh kleethee;
*Have you got the menu?	Ἔχετε τό κατάλογο;
	eheteh toh katalogo
I'd like the key	Θά ἤθελα τό κλειδί;
	tha eethela toh kleethee
I'd like the timetable	Θά ἤθελα τό δρομολόγιο
	tha eethela toh thromologeeo
*I'd like the bill	Θά ἤθελα τό λογαριασμό
	tha eethela toh logareeasmoh
I'd like the receipt	Θά ἤθελα τήν ἀπόδειξη
	tha eethela teen apotheeksee
Where can I get the key?	Ποῦ μπορῶ νά βρῶ τό κλειδί;
	poo boro na vro toh kleethee
Where can I get the suitcase?	Ποῦ μπορῶ νά βρῶ τή βαλίτσα;
	poo boro na vro tee valeetsa
Where can I get the address?	Ποῦ μπορῶ νά βρῶ τή διεύθυνση;
	poo boro na vro tee thee-
	eftheensee

Try adding 'please': παρακαλῶ (parakalo)

The (plural)	masculine	feminine	neuter
the addresses		οἱ διευθύνσεις ee thee- eftheensees	
the apples			τά μῆλα ta meela
the baggage			τά πράγματα ta pragmata
the bills	οἱ λογαριασμοί ee logareeasmee		
the cups of tea			τά τσάγια ta tsaya
the glasses of beer		οἱ μπῦρες ee beeress	
the keys			τά κλειδιά ta kleethya
the menus	οἱ κατάλογοι ee katalogee		
the newspapers		οἱ εφημερίδες ee efeemereethes	
the receipts		οἱ ἀποδείξεις ee apodeeksees	
the sandwiches			τά σάντουϊτς ta sandwich
the suitcases		οἱ βαλίτσες ee valeetses	
the telephone directories	οἱ τηλεφωνικοί κατάλογοι ee teelefoneekee katalogee		
the timetables			τά δρομολόγια ta thromologeea

Important things to remember

- In the plural: most masculine nouns end in -οι (ee)

  most feminine nouns end in -ες (ess) or -εις (eess)

  most neuter nouns end in -α (ah), -ια (ya), or -τα (tah)

- *the* in the plural is:

  οἱ (ee) before masculine and feminine nouns

  τά (tah) before neuter nouns

In phrases beginning: 'Have you got the . . .?'

'I'd like the . . .?

'Where can I get the . . .?'

as in the singular, in the plural, Greek nouns and articles become the object of the sentence and change to form the accusative. Therefore:

	the	noun endings
masculine	οἱ (ee) becomes τούς (toos)	-οι (ee) becomes -ους (oos)
feminine	οἱ (ee) becomes τίς (tees)	(no change)
neuter	(no change)	(no change)

Practise saying and writing these sentences in Greek (masculine nouns are marked * to remind you that *both* the article and the nouns change but remember to change the article with feminine nouns).

Have you got the suitcases?	Ἔχετε τίς βαλίτσες;
	eheteh tees valeetsess
Have you got the keys?	Ἔχετε τά κλειδιά;
	eheteh ta kleethya
*Have you got the bills?	Ἔχετε τούς λογαριασμούς;
	eheteh toos logareeasmoos
I'd like the keys	Θά ἤθελα τά κλειδιά
	tha eethela ta kleethya
I'd like the timetables	Θά ἤθελα τά δρομολόγια
	tha eethela ta thromologeea
*I'd like the bills	Θά ἤθελα τούς λογαριασμούς
	tha eethela toos logareeasmoos
I'd like the newspapers	Θά ἤθελα τίς ἐφημερίδες
	tha eethela tees efeemereethess
Where can I get the keys?	Ποῦ μπορῶ νά βρῶ τά κλειδιά;
	poo boro na vro ta kleethya
Where can I get the newspapers?	Ποῦ μπορῶ νά βρῶ τίς ἐφημερίδες;
	poo boro na vro tees efeemereethess
Where can I get the suitcases?	Ποῦ μπορῶ νά βρῶ τίς βαλίτσες;
	poo boro na vro tees valeetsess

A/AN

a/an	masculine	feminine	neuter
an address		μία διεύθυνση meea thee-eftheensee	
an apple			ἕνα μῆλο enna meeloh
a bill	ἕνας λογαριασμός ennass logareeasmoss		
a cup of tea			ἕνα τσάϊ enna tsa-ee
a glass of beer		μία μπύρα meea beera	
a key			ἕνα κλειδί enna kleethee
a menu	ἕνας κατάλογος ennass katalogoss		
a newspaper		μία ἐφημερίδα meea efeemereetha	
a receipt		μία ἀπόδειξη meea apotheeksee	
a sandwich			ἕνα σάντουιτς enna sandwich
a suitcase		μία βαλίτσα meea valeetsa	
a telephone directory	ἕνας τηλεφωνικός κατάλογος ennass teelefoneekoss katalogoss		
a timetable			ἕνα δρομολόγιο enna thromo-logeeo

Important things to remember

- *A* or *an* is ἕνας (ennass) before a masculine noun
  μία (meea) before a feminine noun
  ἕνα (enna) before a neuter noun
- *Some* or *any* is not translated in Greek, simply say the noun by itself e.g.

  Have you got a key?   Ἔχετε ἕνα κλειδί;
                                eheteh enna kleethee

  Have you got (some) keys?   Ἔχετε κλειδιά;
                                    eheteh kleethya

In phrases beginning: Have you got a/some . . .?
I'd like a/some . . .?
Where can I get a/some . . .?
where Greek nouns and articles become the object of the sentence in the accusative, in the masculine only the word for *a/an* changes from ἕνας (ennass) to ἕνα (enna) and the noun endings change as before (see notes on *the* above). e.g. ἕνας λογαριασμός (ennass logareeasmoss) becomes ἕνα λογαριασμό (enna logareeasmoh).

Practise saying and. writing these sentences in Greek (masculine nouns are marked * to remind you that *both* the article and the noun ending change).

Have you got a receipt?	Ἔχετε μία ἀπόδειξη; eheteh meea apotheeksee
*Have you got a menu?	Ἔχετε ἕνα κατάλογο; eheteh enna katalogo
*I'd like a telephone directory	Θά ἤθελα ἕνα τηλεφωνικό κατάλογο tha eethela enna teelefoneeko katalogo
I'd like some keys	Θά ἤθελα κλειδιά tha eethela kleethya
Where can I get some newspapers?	Ποῦ μπορῶ νά ἀγοράσω ἐφημερίδες; poo boro na agoraso efeemereethess
Where can I get a timetable?	Ποῦ μπορῶ νά βρῶ ἕνα δρομολόγιο; poo boro na vro enna thromologeeo
Is there a menu?	Ὑπάρχει ἕνας κατάλογος; eeparhee ennass katalogoss
Is there a key?	Ὑπάρχει ἕνα κλειδί; eeparhee enna kleethee
Is there a timetable?	Ὑπάρχει ἕνα δρομολόγιο; eeparhee enna thromologeeo
Are there any keys?	Ὑπάρχουν κλειδιά; eeparhoon kleethya
Are there any newspapers?	Ὑπάρχουν ἐφημερίδες; eeparhoon efeemereethess
Are there any sandwiches?	Ὑπάρχουν σάντουϊτς; eeparhoon sandwich

EXTRA PRACTICE WITH 'SOME'

Look at the list below:

the bread	τό ψωμί toh psomee	some bread	ψωμί psomee
the ice-cream	τό παγωτό toh pagotoh	some ice-cream	παγωτό pagotoh
the coffee	ὁ καφές o kafess	some coffee	καφέ kafeh
the sugar	ἡ ζάχαρη ee zaharee	some sugar	ζάχαρη zaharee
the water	τό νερό toh neroh	some water	νερό neroh
the wine	τό κρασί toh krassee	some wine	κρασί krassee

Practise saying and writing these sentences in Greek:

I'd like some bread	Θά ἤθελα ψωμί tha eethela psomee
I'd like some water	Θά ἤθελα νερό tha eethela neroh
Where can I buy some cheese?	Ποῦ μπορῶ νά ἀγοράσω τυρί; poo boro na agoraso teeree
Where can I buy some ice-cream?	Ποῦ μπορῶ νά ἀγοράσω παγωτό; poo boro na agoraso pagoto
Where can I buy some aspirin?	Ποῦ μπορῶ νά ἀγοράσω ἀσπιρίνη; poo boro na agoraso aspeereenee
Have you got some coffee?	Ἔχετε καφέ; eheteh kafeh
Have you got some lemonade?	Ἔχετε λεμονάδα; eheteh lemonatha
Have you got some wine?.	Ἔχετε κρασί; eheteh krassee

THIS AND THAT

There are two words in Greek
αὐτό (this)
afto
ἐκεῖνο (that)
ekeeno
If you don't know the Greek name for an object, just point and say:

Θά ἤθελα αὐτό/ἐκεῖνο	I'd like this/that
tha eethela afto/ekeeno	

HELPING OTHERS

You can help yourself with phrases such as:

I'd like . . . a sandwich	Θά ἤθελα . . . ἕνα σάντουϊτς
	tha eethela . . . enna sandwich
Where can I get . . . a newspaper?	Ποῦ μπορῶ νά ἀγοράσω . . . μία ἐφημερίδα;
	poo boro na agoraso . . . meea efeemereetha
I need . . . a receipt	Χρειάζομαι . . . μία ἀπόδειξη
	hree-azom-eh . . . meea apotheeksee

If you come across a compatriot having trouble making himself or herself understood, you should be able to speak to the Greek person on their behalf.

Note that it is not necessary to say the words for *he* αὐτός (aftos) *she* αὐτή (aftee) and *I* ἐγώ (egoh) in Greek unless you want to emphasise them e.g. *He'll* have a beer and *I'll* have a glass of wine.

He'd like a sandwich	Θά ἤθελε ἕνα σάντουϊτς
	tha eethell-eh enna sandwich
She'd like a sandwich	Θά ἤθελε ἕνα σάντουϊτς
	tha eethell-eh enna sandwich
Where can he get a newspaper?	Ποῦ μπορεῖ νά ἀγοράσει μία ἐφημερίδα;
	poo bor-ee na agorass-ee meea ef-eemehr-eetha

Where can she get a newspaper?	Ποὺ μπορεῖ νά ἀγοράσει μία ἐφημερίδα;
	poo bor-*ee* na agorass-ee meea ef-eemer-*eetha*
He needs a receipt	Χρειάζεται μία ἀπόδειξη
	hree-*azet*-eh meea apo-theek-see
She needs a receipt	Χρειάζεται μία ἀπόδειξη
	hree-*azet*-eh meea apo-theek-see

You can also help a couple or a group if they are having difficulties. The Greek words for *they* are αὐτές (aft*ess*) for women, αὐτοί (aft*ee*) for men, but they are usually left out altogether. Look at the verb ending.

They'd like some cheese	Θά θέλανε τυρί
	tha thell-aneh teer-*ee*
Where can they get some aspirins?	Ποὺ μποροῦν νά ἀγοράσουν ἀσπιρίνες;
	poo bor-*oon* na agorass-oon aspeereen-ess
They need some water	Χρειάζονται νερό
	hree-*azon*-deh neroh

What about the two of you? The word for *we* is ἐμεῖς (em*eess*) but what is really important is to change the verb ending.

We'd like some wine	Θά θέλαμε κρασί
	tha thellam-eh krass-*ee*
Where can we get some aspirins?	Ποὺ μποροῦμε νά ἀγοράσουμε ἀσπιρίνες;
	poo bor-*oom*-eh na agorass-oom-eh aspeereen-ess
We need a beer	Χρειαζόμαστε μία μπύρα
	hree-*azom*-asteh meea beer-a

Overleaf is a checklist for these useful phrase starters:

Θά ἤθελα . . .	I'd like . . .
tha *ee*thela	
Θά ἤθελε . . .	He'd/she'd like . . .
tha *ee*thel-eh	
Θά θέλαμε . . .	We'd like . . .
tha the*lam*-eh	
Θά θέλανε . . .	They'd like . . .
tha thel-*aneh*	
Ποῦ μπορῶ νά βρῶ . . .	Where can I get . . .?
poo bor*o* na vro	
Ποῦ μπορεί νά βρεῖ . . .	Where can he/she get . . .?
poo bor*ee* na vree	
Ποῦ μπορούμε νά βρούμε . . .	Where can we get . . .?
poo bor*oo*me na vr*oo*me	
Ποῦ μπορούν νά βρούν . . .	Where can they get . . .?
poo bor*oon* na vroon	
Χρειάζομαι . . .	I need . . .
hree-*azom*-eh	
Χρειάζεται . . .	He/she needs . . .
hree-*azet*-eh	
Χρειαζόμαστε . . .	We need . . .
hree-azom-asteh	
Χρειάζονται . . .	They need . . .
hree-*azon*-deh	

MORE PRACTICE

Look at the opposite page and see how many different sentences you can make up, using the various points of information given earlier in this section.

	singular	plural
ashtray	τασάκι (n)	τασάκια
	tas*ah*kee	tas*ah*kya
bag	τσάντα (f)	τσάντες
	ts*a*nda	tsandess
book	βιβλίο (n)	βιβλία
	veevl*ee*o	veevl*ee*a
car	αὐτοκίνητο (n)	αὐτοκίνητα
	aftok*ee*neeto	aftok*ee*neeta
chair	καρέκλα (f)	καρέκλες
	kar*eh*kla	kar*eh*kless
chemist	φαρμακείο (n)	φαρμακεία
	farmak*ee*o	farmak*ee*a
cigarette	τσιγάρο (n)	τσιγάρα
	tseeg*a*ro	tseeg*a*ra
driver	ὁδηγός (m)	ὁδηγοί
	othee*goss*	othee*gee*
fruit	φροῦτο (n)	φροῦτα
	fr*oo*toh	fr*oo*tah
glass	ποτήρι (n)	ποτήρια
	pot*ee*ree	pot*ee*rya
ice-cream	παγωτό (n)	παγωτά
	pagot*o*	pagot*a*
olive	ἐλιά (f)	ἐλιές
	ell*ya*	ellyess
post-office	ταχυδρομεῖο (n)	ταχυδρομεῖα
	taheethrom*ee*o	taheethrom*ee*a
room	δωμάτιο (n)	δωμάτια
	thom*a*teeo	thom*a*teea
salad	σαλάτα (f)	σαλάτες
	sal*a*ta	sal*a*tess
station	σταθμός (m)	σταθμοί
	stath*moss*	stath*mee*
telephone	τηλέφωνο (n)	τηλέφωνα
	teel*e*fono	teel*e*fona
ticket	εἰσιτήριο (n)	εἰσιτήρια
	eeseet*ee*rio	eeseet*ee*rya
tinned food	κονσέρβα (f)	κονσέρβες
	kons*e*rva	kons*e*rvess
tomato	ντομάτα (f)	ντομάτες
	dom*a*ta	dom*a*tess

Index

Arthur Eperon
Travellers' Italy

A whole variety of holiday routes to guarantee that you eat, drink, explore and relax in the places the Italians themselves would choose. The best places to sample local speciality foods and wines, spectacular scenery, facts the history books won't tell you, as well as the magnificent beaches and art treasures you'd expect Arthur Eperon is one of the best-known travel writers in Europe and has an extensive knowledge of Italy and its food and wine. With an introduction by Frank Bough,

Travellers' France

Six major routes across France, taking in the best restaurants and hotels, visiting the most interesting out-of-the-way places. This detailed and up-to-the-minute handbook is for the traveller who wants more out of France than a mad dash down the motorway Each of the six routes across the country is illustrated with a specially-commissioned two-colour map, and includes a host of information on where to eat and drink, where to take children, where to stay, and how to get the most out of the towns and countryside.

John Slater
Just Off for the Weekend
Slater's hotel guide

The bestselling author of *Just Off the Motorway* has selected more than a hundred places to stay, with details of what to see and walks to take, specially recommended pubs and restaurants – and all within a Friday evening's drive from one of England's big cities. With an introduction by Anna Ford.

Companion Language Dictionaries

English – Français	French – Anglais
English – Deutsch	German – Englisch
English – Español	Spanish – Inglés
English – Italiano	Italian – Inglese

These pocket bilingual dictionaries have been especially designed for use by both English *and* French, German, Spanish and Italian speakers and are suitable for tourists, business travellers and students up to approximately O level. Each dictionary contains about 10,000 headwords; each entry contains a minimum of useful grammatical information such as gender of nouns, cases with German verbs etc. There is a pronunciation guide to both the foreign language and English headwords.

Harrap's New Pocket French and English Dictionary

The classic French/English and English/French reference for students and travellers, this edition contains some 4,500 entries in each language, including all the principal words in current use – recent additions to both languages, scientific terms, tourist expressions. Entries also contain phonetic renderings and examples of idiomatic use.

A Multilingual Commercial Dictionary

Some 3,000 words and phrases in common commercial use are listed in English, French, German, Spanish and Portuguese followed by their translation in the other languages. The equivalent American expression is also included where relevant. Simple to use and invaluable for everyday reference, the dictionary covers terms used throughout banking, accounting, insurance, shipping, export and import and international trade.

Now available to accompany this phrase book
A specially recorded, 60-minutes

Audio cassette

Why a cassette?

This cassette has been produced to enable phrase book users to
become familiar with

- the pronunciation and intonation of Greek, preferably before
  leaving for Greece
- the pronunciation guide provided in the book
- the likely reactions to their questions in Greek

What is on the cassette?

Selected parts of nearly all sections of the phrase book have
been recorded by a native speaker. There is no separate script:
the recording tells you which page in the phrase book to turn to.
It is ideal for using in the car or for listening to while doing jobs
around the house.

   ALL LIKELY REACTIONS, and the key phrases to understand,
are recorded so that you can get used to listening to them.

   All other phrases (WHAT TO SAY) can be repeated out loud,
and pauses have been left on the cassette so that you can
imitate the speaker without having to stop the tape.

This cassette has been recorded and produced by PRINTAWAY
LIMITED for PAN BOOKS LIMITED and is *only* available from

Printaway Publishing,

Poplar Lane,

Leith, Edinburgh EH6 7HD

Tel: Edinburgh (031) 551 2549

Price £5.00 (incl VAT, P&P)
Also available in French, Spanish, Italian and German.